# Walls Have Feelings
## architecture, film and the city

Every day films are made in cities, buildings and rooms, and every day architects and urbanists make decisions about cities, buildings and rooms. Their skills are addressed to the same subject but they inhabit different worlds. Now, for the first time, this book brings the insights, methodologies and visions of film to the practice of architecture.

*Walls Have Feelings* uses films to reassess post-war architecture and urbanism in London, Paris and New York. It takes a close and provocative look at classic films from the Forties, Fifties and Sixties, including *Alfie*, *Passport to Pimlico*, *Mary Poppins*, *Repulsion* and *Rosemary's Baby*. In particular, the  book examines the equivocal portrayal of women and sex to provide new and surprising insights into the impact of 'technical' decisions – from road building to damp penetration – that currently affect our lives. This book interconnects the detail, the interior, and the city at large.

*Walls Have Feelings* poses unanswered questions from our immediate past, crucial for the future of the city: what was the cultural mind-set leading to the triumph of Brutalism? What is the urban and domestic impact of large-scale office building? Are there alternatives to the planners' city of objects? And why does your flat leak?

This book uniquely brings to bear questions of urgent cultural relevance on critical design decisions. As such, it is of as much importance to architects, planners and students of design as to students of cultural history, geography and all enthusiasts of cities and of film.

**Katherine Shonfield** is teacher of History and Theory in the Department of Architecture at South Bank University. She is a partner in the architectural practice Shonfield and Williams Architects, is Deputy Editor of the *Journal of Architecture* (Routledge) and has a weekly column in the *Architects' Journal*.

# Walls Have Feelings

## architecture, film and the city

Katherine Shonfield

London and New York

First published 2000
by Routledge
11 New Fetter Lane, London EC4P 4EE

Simultaneously published in the USA and Canada
by Routledge
29 West 35th Street, New York, NY 10001

*Routledge is an imprint of the Taylor & Francis Group*

Typeset in Galliard by Keystroke, Jacaranda Lodge, Wolverhampton
Printed and bound in Great Britain by St Edmundsbury Press, Bury St Edmunds,
Suffolk

*British Library Cataloguing in Publication Data*
A catalogue record for this book is available from the British Library

*Library of Congress Cataloging in Publication Data*
Shonfield. Katherine, 1954–
    Walls have feelings : architecture, film and the city / Katherine Shonfield.
        p.   cm.
    Includes bibliographical references and index.
    1. Cities and towns in motion pictures.   2. Architecture in motion pictures.   3. Motion
    picture locations.   I. Title.

    PN1995.9.C513 S535 2000
    791.43′621732—dc21                                                                00-032216

ISBN 0–415–23542–1 (pbk)
ISBN 0–415–23541–3 (hbk)

For Roman Williams
How wonderful life is now you're in the world

# Contents

# How to use this book

This book can be read in any order, from back to front, middle to end, as separate sections and as single chapters.

The proviso is that, like a film, it needs the reader to 'run with' its narrative for the duration. To begin to get into its insights you need to suspend some disbelief.

The aim of the book is to get at a number of questions about architecture, construction and the city through using film. And the point is to bring knowledge from fiction and film to challenge professional assumptions about the way architecture and the city invariably 'work'. *Walls Have Feelings* is divided into three parts, which, if you read them consecutively, move from the particular to the general. The first is *The Detail*, the middle section, *The Interior*, and the final section is *The City*.

Readers with different interests can go straight for the parts that are important to them. If you are interested in film first, and architecture second, read Chapter 1, especially the second part which looks at parallels between the contrasting film aesthetics of an Ealing comedy, *Passport to Pimlico*, an example of the British New Wave, *It Happened Here*, and *Beat Girl*, a 1960s' camp B-feature with a concrete interior. Read also Chapter 3, on Polanski's *Repulsion* and *Rosemary's Baby*; Chapter 4, concerning two films about offices in Manhattan, *The Apartment*, and *Sabrina Fair*, and two great films of 1960s' London: *Alfie* and *Darling*; Chapter 5, about Jean-Luc Godard's *Two or Three Things I Know About Her*, and Chapter 6, on *L.A. Story*, and three more London films: *Mary Poppins*, *The Chain*, about moving house, and *Four in the Morning*, about the River Thames.

If you are interested in themes of gender, go to Chapter 3, an essay on two films which use the metaphor of the interior of the female body and the interior of an apartment; go to Chapter 4, which deals with the interrelationship of decorative femininity, the interior and the office in the 1960s; and Chapter 5, which is about the way the city of Paris, its interiors and the figure of a prostitute are metaphorically intertwined.

If you are interested in London, then you should go to Chapter 4, for issues emerging from the city's rebuilding in the 1960s, and Chapter 6, for discussion of alternative imagery from fiction for envisioning London as a whole. For issues surrounding London's post-war construction, go to Chapter 1 which deals with Brutalism, and Chapter 2, which is about building failure.

If your interest is building technology and its cultural implications, go to Chapter 2, which is an attempt to reassess assumptions in everyday building construction, and Chapter 3, for further discussion on permeability and the cultural imagery of technical literature.

## A summary of the contents

**Chapter 1**: *How Brutalism defeated picturesque populism: parallels in film and architecture* is set in a post-war Britain anxious about its borders. It draws parallels between the content and aesthetic of British picturesque modernism of the late 1940s, and a classic post-war comedy from London's Ealing studio; it contrasts this with Brutalism and the New Wave monochrome aesthetic of British cinema in the early 1960s.

 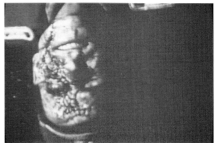

**Chapter 2**: *Why does your flat leak?* uses fictions to start to probe building failures normally the province of the technical, in particular permeability. It undoes some of the blindness that comes with accepted ways of looking at construction, such as the Practical, the Common Sense and the Scientific.

In **Chapter 3**, *These walls have feelings: the interiors of* Repulsion *and* Rosemary's Baby, the architectural interiors in which these two films are set and the bodies of their heroines are interchangeable. This chapter reads these films against technical anxieties about construction, and, again, its permeability, played out in London and New York.

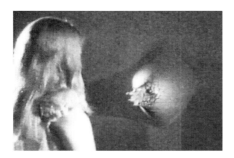

**Chapter 4**: *Wives and lovers: the 1960s' office interior:* Alfie, The Apartment *and* Darling, is about another interchangeability: when decorative women substitute for the decorative interior. It looks at the huge offices of London and New York, and the presentation of women within them, as opportunities for a new promiscuity.

In **Chapter 5**: *Free circulation = free copulation: women and roads in* Nana *and* Two or Three Things I Know About Her, both novel and film are about major road building projects which encompass and define the city. Like *Repulsion* and *Rosemary's Baby*, the body of the woman is a metaphor: this time, not just for the interior, but for the city as a whole.

**Chapter 6**: *Against the city of objects:* Our Mutual Friend, Mary Poppins, L.A. Story, considers how the metaphors of post-war planning in London enact the need to contain and delineate the city by exclusion. It looks at alternatives from film and the novel to open up future possibilities for new ways to comprehend the city as a whole.

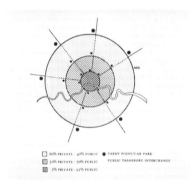

The **Endpiece** is the most academic part of the book. In it I trace the theories and methods the rest of the book uses, and propose some new ways of using fiction in general to interpret architecture and the city. In a sense it is a key to threads which run through the chapters – but you do not need to read it to understand the rest of the book. Each chapter and part can, and does, stand alone.

**Part one:** The Detail

# Chapter 1
## How Brutalism defeated picturesque populism:
parallels in film and architecture

It is hardly possible to overdramatise the effects that the wholesale adoption of the Brutalist style – with its trademark bleak, uncovered, grey concrete – has had on the landscape of London. Together with its architectural sister, system building, and the monuments of the office boom, the tower blocks and new housing estates have transformed our experience of the city.

This book starts with an attempt to shed light on a question still to be answered, and which remains as urgent today as much as in the aftermath of the 1960s. What made the British reject out of hand their traditions of gentle adaptation and picturesque embellishment, and take on so comprehensively an architectural style that was self-consciously ugly and ideologically generated? The reason for the continued urgency is an apparently never-ending schism between how the general public perceive the after-effects of Brutalism, and the immovable conviction by architects that this period was their heyday. For architects, this was both the last time the profession could transform the everyday lives of the many on a concerted scale; and also the last time a style had social and political purpose, imbued with architectural integrity. As for the public, they just hate it.

The fall-out persists into this century. Before the public can give any large-scale commitment again to architects, a line of mutual understanding has to be drawn under the circumstances which generated the styles and forms of this period.

To begin a new exploration in this chapter, I try to do two things. The first is to suggest that *the defence (or otherwise) of the border* is an overriding theme which allows an understanding of the interconnection of political, social, architectural and cultural activities in the decades preceding the 1960s. The second is to look for insights outside architecture, specifically in film, and to seeks parallels and commentary on the demise of the picturesque aesthetic in British cinema of the same period.

The picturesque architecture of the 1940s and early 1950s is currently enjoying new interest. Its most well-known example is the buildings of the Festival of Britain. This was a national festival put on six years after the end of war, in 1951, which temporarily occupied the area of the South Bank of the Thames directly opposite London's West End. I consider this against the once again popular Ealing comedy, *Passport to Pimlico*. The Festival buildings embody what's been seen either as a happy marriage or an abominable birth. They are the result of the fusion between two apparently opposed traditions: the rigours of international modernism and the English picturesque tradition, a tradition which implies design first and foremost in terms of the composition of a series of visual pictures.[1] In film, I suggest, there was a broad, and perhaps equally popular equivalent: the Ealing comedy. These quintessentially English films emanated from the Ealing Studio in west London, and were at their best in this period. They epitomise the spirit of post-war Britain and London in particular: a hybrid world where there was a simultaneous longing for radical change and tangible continuity. As if to express this strange contradiction, the comedies feature gangs of lovable robbers, charming and funny murderers and, in the case of *Passport to Pimlico*, sensible and conventional anarchists.

Both architecture and film began to go markedly out of fashion in the second post-war decade. They were replaced with monochrome, and supposedly true-to-life genres: Brutalism's parallel was Britain's version of the New Wave in cinema.[2] Angst-ridden, alienated loners replace chirpy communities. Remorseless realism replaces happy endings. This is both an exploration of parallels between their aesthetics and their preoccupations, and an attempt to cast insight from architecture on cinema and vice versa. The preoccupations of post-war architecture set the scene at the beginning of the chapter, and cinematic themes are taken up in the second half.

To allow speculation between the social, political architectural and filmic material, I use a fictional motif. It is extrapolated from the anthropologist Mary Douglas' theory of the origins of pollution taboos. It is described in more detail in this book's *Endpiece*. The point of using this work is to arrive at a kind of common *currency* which allows us to move between the various areas of exploration. As I indicated above, this concerns the idea of *the defence of the border*. Borders hold in what is defined and pure. And a set of characteristics allows identification of the pure in contrast to the hybrid. The pure can have a line drawn clearly round it. The pure can be reduced to an original set of classes. The borders between the *form* of the pure and the *formlessness* outside it, are well defined and self-evident.

The idea of the hybrid is the opposite of the pure. The hybrid straddles two or more classes; its edges are unclear, and difficult to delineate, to draw a line around. The hybrid doesn't have an identifiable, categorisable form. The hybrid obscures the possibility of its reduction to an original set of parts or classes. The hybrid transgresses the edges of established forms. The pure and the hybrid polarise the two tendencies in British post-war architecture. And these two tendencies can be personified in two iconic buildings, the Skylon and Hunstanton School.

The Skylon (Fig. 1.1) was a vertical structure built for the Festival of Britain in 1950, and designed by two competition-winning architectural students, Philip Powell and Hidalgo Moya. Hunstanton School, another competition winner designed

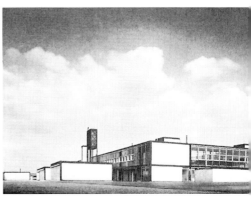

**1.1** Drawing by Hidalgo Moya of the Skylon, Festival of Britain, London (1951): Powell and Moya.

**1.2** Hunstanton School, Norfolk, UK (1956): Alison and Peter Smithson.

by Alison and Peter Smithson, was one of the first Brutalist buildings completed six years late, and crucial to Brutalism's identification as a new and challenging style (Fig. 1.2).

The presentation drawing shows the Skylon as part of a picturesque composition complete with moody sky, passing boat and Victorian railway bridge. It also shows that it is meant to be experienced as seamless. Skylon was clad in steel panelling but the edges between components are suppressed, the line between distinct constructional parts fuzzed. The structure connecting the Skylon to the ground is similarly made invisible. The structure seems to float intangibly: the point at its bottom end means it can never sit on the ground like a structure that could be categorised as 'tower'. Skylon, like its equally popular post-war namesake, Nylon, is a hybrid.

By contrast, Hunstanton is pure. While it completely lacks what became the Brutalist tag, uncovered concrete, Hunstanton is a textbook of the characteristics behind the *idea* of this most self-conscious of styles. Hunstanton declares the distinct categories of its construction throughout. The edge is clearly underlined between brick panel and steel frame. It is equally clear that the frame not the bricks holds the building up. The purity of its form, expressed by the parts that make up the building, is as transparent from inside as it is from outside (Fig. 1.3).

No attempt is made to cover up any edge, or obscure any category. In this interpretation, Brutalism defends borders; it upholds the unpolluted and pure against the hybrid characteristics of the Festival Style.

The problem, though, as ever, is how to relate these specifically *visual* aspects of architecture to broader social and political ideas, that is, the context for these two

**1.3** Interior of hall at Hunstanton School, Norfolk, UK (1956): Alison and Peter Smithson.

markedly different ways of making buildings. Mary Douglas herself establishes terms which cross over from the material to the social. She characterises four varieties of social 'pollution', all associated with defence of the border. They are threats to external boundaries; threats to internal lines within a social system; threats to margins of the lines defining a social system; and the fourth variety is 'danger from internal contradiction, when some of the basic postulates are denied by other basic postulates, so that at certain points the system seems to be at war with itself'.[3] All these kinds of social pollution described directly threaten the coherent *delineation* of a particular community, its defining edges and rules. They can be used to understand perceived threats to the architectural community itself after the end of the second world war, and to characterise those threats as a battle of the pure versus the hybrid.

The architectural historian and critic, Reyner Banham, is acknowledged as the official chronicler of Brutalism. He himself along with Alison and Peter Smithson was a member of the self-styled Independent Group, an avant-garde of artists and architects, formed in London in 1952. They originated both the idea and the term 'Brutalism'. It is from the activities and concerns of the Independent Group that he identifies the genesis of the style in his 1966 book *The New Brutalism*.[4] For Banham, it's clear that what the profession understood as 'architecture' was under threat both from the Festival Style, and also from widespread local authority architecture of the immediate post-war years,

> a style based on a sentimental regard for nineteenth century vernacular usages, with pitched roofs, brick or rendered walls, window boxes, balconies, pretty paintwork, a tendency to elaborate woodwork detailing and freely picturesque grouping.[5]

He goes on:

> The younger generation, viewing these works, had the depressing sense that the drive was going out of Modern Architecture, its pure dogma being diluted by politicians and compromisers who had lost their intellectual nerve.[6]

The functionalist principles of modernist design were handed down from the European masters of the early years of the 20th century. These principles were, by the end of the 1930s, the established rules of architectural practice. Going back to Douglas, it was these rules – machine aesthetic and anti-decorative in appearance – which defined the internal lines, the borders, of architectural aesthetics as a system. And it is these rules, referred to by Banham as modern architecture's 'pure dogma', which were perceived as polluted and transgressed by the post-war hybrid style.

It was not just the new style's literal transgression of pure modernist lines with 'elaborate woodwork detailing and freely picturesque grouping' that threatened professional purity. It was the very fact of the *hybridity* of this new, debased, modernist style. Douglas' statement that pollution threatens when there is 'danger from internal contradiction . . . so that . . . the system seems to be at war with itself' is particularly apposite here. Banham does not identify this as a problem of confrontation of one style with another. Rather, his concern is with the *debasement* of the identifying characteristics of modernism by the new style, which in the public mind was and continues to be associated with 'modern architecture'. The problem, in other words, is the hybrid.

It's important that Banham places Brutalism's ruthless pursuit of 'honesty' in architecture in the tradition of the great modernist rule-makers.

> The morality that approved the raw concrete of the Unité (of Le Corbusier) could equally well approve the use that Mies van der Rohe had made of steel, glass and brick in the campus buildings at Illinois.[7]

Reflecting its 19th-century origins as an idea in the work of John Ruskin and others, architectural 'honesty' is characterised as not covering things up. In other words, the *moral* connotations of the 'honest' are directly transferred onto the architecture. True architecture is created out of a series of bold, and bald, statements of what material abuts what, what structure supports what. How the building is *revealed* to have been made is all important. So this is inevitably an aesthetic preoccupied with construction. It is above all at the junction between two building elements that the architect has the choice between an aesthetic of hiding, covering up how the building is put together, and one of revealing it. If we associate the idea of the *honest* with the *pure*, the characteristics of Brutalist architecture slip into place. These include the use of materials that can be called 'elemental' rather than hybrid, invented ones – as in concrete, and not plastic. It means the emphatic underlining of the identifiable origins of materials – as in never colouring painting or rendering over concrete. It means the accentuation of the undisguised edge to a building component, such as recessed joints between individual bricks.

What is intriguing about this particular architectural aesthetic is that these are essentially arbitrary formal qualities, but they come not just to *signify* honesty, but to be understood as honest *in and of themselves*, the moral essence of honesty, as Ruskin himself would have argued. Despite the best intentions of the movement's promoters, revealed in Peter Smithson's well-known statement of 1957,

> Any discussion of Brutalism will miss the point if it does not take into account Brutalism's attempt to be objective about 'reality' – the cultural objectives of society, its urges, its techniques and so on. Brutalism tries to face up to a mass producing society and drag a rough poetry out of the confused and powerful forces which are at work.[8]

the aesthetic signifiers of Brutalist architecture move beyond referent to subject. What this means is that 'morality' in construction is proof to the profession of the internal consistency of its own architectural language, and the firmness of its own closely guarded social distinctions, its 'internal lines'. Through this sleight of hand, where formal characteristics are inherently honest, it becomes possible to prove a morality, a worthiness in architecture *completely independently* of its social impact on the external world.[9] And this means that an architect can be well satisfied that his architecture is *moral* despite perceptions on the part of users and the general public that it is *a travesty of morality*. This goes some way to explain the profession's astounding deafness to the outcry against Brutalist-derived aesthetics which started in the 1970s.

Banham, writing in *The New Brutalism*, conveys the feeling that the post-war decade is a period of political, as well as architectural, muddle, and indeed muddiness. The war-time experiences of the designers of the first new towns and the Festival of Britain 'had served to confuse their aims and blunt their intellectual attack'.[10] In particular, Banham implicates the championing by the London County Council, which was the largest architectural practice in post-war Britain, of the decorated modernism he calls 'People's Detailing'. He intimates that the style was associated with the Communist caucus within its architect's department, and that it was seen as the equivalent to Socialist Realism, the Communist Party's officially sanctioned aesthetic at the time. This is the political context for the unprecedented vilification by Reyner Banham of the respected editor of *Architectural Review*, J.M. Richards, for his book on the English suburb, *The Castles on the Ground*.[11]

Banham calls the book

> a specimen example of war-time home thoughts from abroad, a sentimental evocation (written in Cairo) of the virtues and less damaging vices of Victorian suburbia . . . this book in particular was regarded . . . as a blank betrayal of everything that the Modern Architecture was supposed to stand for.[12]

The betrayal was personal. Before the war, Richards had been one of the most vociferous and influential of exponents of European modernism. *The Castles on the Ground* is a persuasive argument for an architecture of 'the animating spirit of popular sanction' – popular architecture, as we would now call it. Such an architecture should stand against both 'private connoisseurship and technological narcissism',[13] and the notion of an avant-garde. And writing on the avant-garde, Richards says that:

> we can only progress democratically at a speed which does not outpace the slow growth of the public's understanding, in particular its assimilation of social and technical change.[14]

Richards' argument favours the suburb. For him it is the formal, architectural expression of a democratic (i.e. popularly led) assimilation of such technological and social change. In fact, his aesthetic support for the suburban *form* rests precisely on the fact that it is a hybrid, and does not fit into one or the other accepted planning category:

> It is a mistake to think of the suburb as either the town spaced out or the country packed close . . . the suburb is not primarily a mechanism, nor is it in any sense a modification of something previously existing; it is a world peculiar to itself and – as with a theatre's drop scene – before and behind it there is nothing.[15]

The theatrical metaphor – 'before and behind it there is nothing' – reveals not only that Richards sees the suburb as a hybrid, but as a form *where issues of honesty are entirely irrelevant.* There is an implied political association between arguments for Socialist Realism, with the promotion of hybrid, and fuzzy forms – whether architectural or urban. This is made clear when Richards writes:

> What the mass of the Russian public – like the mass of English suburban residents – require of their architecture is a sense that it represents what they themselves are striving after and it must do so in a language they already understand . . . In fact for all their distance apart, geographically and spiritually, Moscow and Metroland have this in common, that architecture is to them not an art form to be accepted or rejected according to the rules of aesthetic taste. It is a symbol of what is real and tangible in an uncertain world.[16]

So, this interpretation of *the defence of the border* provides a way of understanding in parallel three sources of disquiet which all colour London's post-war architectural world. The first is to do with form. It concerns the urge to establish an unequivocal set of rules to delineate what is acceptable in built, physical architecture. The second is social. It is the architectural profession's preoccupation with rules defining and delineating its sense of itself. And the third is the wider post-war political context – of flux, uncertainty and change.

On a much broader international scale than architectural infighting at the London County Council during the 1940s, this period was a time of confusion, of shifting social and political borders. The changing status of Russia within a six-year period from foe (1939–42) to ally (1942–48) to foe again (1948 onwards) affected everyone in the West, not just Communist Party members and fellow travellers. It meant certainties of good/evil, east/west, progressive/reactionary were inevitably much more wobbly than in the 20 years preceding the second world war. The proceedings of the 1949 meeting of CIAM,[17] an international organisation of architects which was by now the established voice of the European modernist ascendancy, reflect the three parallel disputes over a sense of order, outlined above, in this wider context.

Siegfried Gideon, the greatest of the chroniclers of modernism, chaired a meeting of the committee on aesthetics – an issue raised for the first time at the previous year's meeting at Bridgwater in Britain.[18] There, Richards and the MARS[19] group (an association of British modernists) had posed this challenging question for modernist faith:

> What can architects do to take into account those qualities in building that have, at the present moment, a symbolic or emotional significance for ordinary people so that architecture shall remain an art in whose adventures they can share?

The 1949 response was an uncompromising appeal to the honest and authentic:[20]

> CIAM cannot accept class distinctions nor a lowering of artistic standards for sentimental or political reasons. On the contrary we believe that anyone not perverted by false education is capable of appreciating true values in art.

The representatives from Eastern Europe, an architectural couple appropriately called the Syrkuses, were involved in the reconstruction plan for Warsaw, based, in the centre at least, on the meticulous replication of pre-war urban order. They confirmed the convergence of the political motive with the revision of modernist architectural form. Their argument developed the implications of J.M. Richards' book by directly challenging the principle of revealed honesty in construction:

> Art belongs to the people and is understandable by the people . . . Construction is but a skeleton. It has great interest for the anatomist, but for the rest it only becomes beautiful when it is covered with fine muscle and lovely skin. We had nothing else to offer at the time when CIAM began, and so we made a fetish of the skeleton.[21]

This was the Communist Party line: the architectural version of Socialist Realism in the arts, and a reversal of earlier Party support for the modernist avant-garde. Joan Ockman documents how it was soon to be reversed, yet again:

> Five years later, after Stalin's death, the Syrkuses would return to the functionalist line newly rehabilitated under Nikita Khruschev, and in 1956 Szymon Syrkus would travel to CIAM's meeting in Dubrovnik to undertake the necessary revanchism.[22]

The undeniable political corruption behind changes of architectural stance, such as those which Ockman documents, and the resulting final disillusionment of progressives with Communism on the invasion of Hungary by Russia in 1956, served only to confirm the moral worth of the architecture and the character of those professionals who had steadfastly adhered to 'honest' rules all the way through. The assumption was established that there is an irradicable correspondence between honest constructional aesthetic, pure rules and a transparent, uncorruptible political position. It continues to this day.

## Hybrid Ealing vs. pure new wave – three London films

The parallel in this second part of the chapter is between the circumstances of Brutalism's rejection of the hybrid, picturesque style, and the emergence of British

New Wave cinema, and its own break with the picturesque manifestations of the Ealing Studio. I speculate on the aesthetics and the content of a contemporary change in British cinema, embodied in two great films about London, *Passport to Pimlico* (directed by Henry Cornelius, 1948) and *It Happened Here* (directed by Kevin Brownlow and Andrew Mollo, 1956–63).

It may seem at first sight eccentric to compare *Passport to Pimlico*, one of the most popular British film comedies ever, with *It Happened Here*, a film that was initiated by a 16-year-old and an 18-year-old in 1956 and was finished seven years later in 1963, and is so disturbing that it remained banned from British television until the early 1980s. But I have deliberately chosen two films to look at in correspondence with the two eras under examination, the 1940s, and the second half of the 1950s, and which are both set in London. They also both tackle the disquieting question: what if the outcome of the war were different? In *Passport to Pimlico* during the immediate post-war aftermath, the inner London district of Pimlico discovers that it is not British at all, but part of the ancient Duchy of Burgundy. In *It Happened Here*, Britain has been defeated by Germany and is under Nazi occupation.

The post-war preoccupation with the nature of nationality and the need for a popular recognition of nationhood is an underlying theme of J.M. Richards' *The Castles on the Ground*. War-time propaganda obviously made it necessary for national identification to be associated unequivocally with the Allies. *Passport to Pimlico* should be seen against the background of Britain Standing Alone propaganda of the first years of the war; the need to frame what was being fought for in terms of protecting what it meant to be British, and the USSR's shifting status in these years from enemy to friend and back again. The great Ealing comedies of the end of the 1940s, *Passport to Pimlico*, *Whisky Galore* and *Kind Hearts and Coronets*, all obsessively explore the hybrid and elusive qualities of Britishness. It is characteristic of them that they combine, like the style and content of the Festival of Britain itself, outrageously imaginative future possibilities with a quaint respect for a quirky, irregular way of life, which signifies a kind of unchanging familiarity. In the Festival this saw the juxtaposition of the still startling futuristic Skylon and Dome of Discovery, with content such as an embroidered relief mural by the Women's Institute entitled 'The Country Wife'.[23] A peculiar graphic style signals this merging of apparently distinct positions. It appears in the advertisement for *Kind Hearts and Coronets* (Fig. 1.4) and is familiar from *The Castles on the Ground* (Fig. 1.5); a graphic with its very own compromised edges and broken lines.

*Passport to Pimlico* captures London's immediate post-war mood. The people of Pimlico are fed up to the back teeth with all the state restrictions remaining from the war economy, such as trade curbs, food rationing and curfews. Some treasure and ancient documents are unearthed on a bomb site which prove Pimlico to be part of

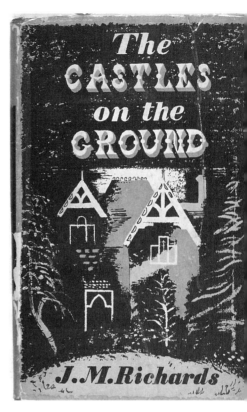

**1.4** *Kind Hearts and Coronets* (1949): Poster.

**1.5** *The Castles on the Ground* (1946): Front cover by John Piper.

the independent French Duchy of Burgundy. After a period of freedom, confrontation with the authorities, and a blockade, Pimlico renegotiates itself as part of Britain. The heat wave that has been continuous since Pimlico was declared part of continental Europe, promptly ends with a massive downpour.

In the aftermath of Pimlico's transformation into Burgundy, a series of social and architectural borders are transgressed. The change to continental, sultry weather turns the squalid back yards of the inner city into a site for romance where a female citizen of Pimlico and the young Burgundian duke kiss. In the new Pimlico two defining characteristics of Britishness are questioned: sexual reticence and grotty back yards. The assailant is a European, literally a category of person which had been out-of-bounds for the duration of the war. On becoming Burgundians, the Pimlico citizens initiate after-hours drinking, free dancing and singing: all social activities, then as now, contained by licence in the UK. They lift rationing and trade restrictions.

The British state's response to these transgressions provides the comedy's most disturbing, and surprising image: Pimlico is cordoned off with a barbed wire fence, a physical, national border where passport controls are promptly installed. The source of all this containment and control of daily life is consistently shown as a bureaucratic, impersonal state. Exactly who has propriety over definitions of nationality is questioned. Nationality defined through *delineation*, the imposition of lines which define pure and impure is particularly called into doubt. Images of Londoners throwing food over the Pimlico barbed wire are a pointed reminder of the Berlin Airlift of the same year, when the non-Communist zones of Berlin were impelled to receive their supplies by air (Fig. 1.6). The trauma of the German capital is, rather touchingly, played out on the fabric of London, its declared enemy only two years before the film was made. The overt analogy suggests that people are pawns and victims of manipulation of notions of nationality in both cities.

**1.6** *Passport to Pimlico* (1948): Throwing food over the border to blockaded Pimlico.

Notwithstanding the best attempts of Churchill's 1946 speech to announce an Iron Curtain across Europe, intent on the rigid redefinition of lines of national identity, the spirit of post-war resistance to categorical delineations of nationality is neatly summed up in *Passport to Pimlico*. Betty Warren, a Pimlico grocer's wife, declares:

We always were English, and we will always be English, and it's just because we're English we're sticking out for our right to be Burgundians.

The state of Englishness paradoxically occurs only when the district becomes ersatz France by becoming Burgundy – a mythic place in between the two, neither France nor England. True Englishness exists only when nationality is smeared.

Consequent on its cat-and-mouse game with border and transgression, Pimlico blossoms into a new series of architecturally hybrid (for Britain) adaptations of the street: markets unrestricted by licence, and pavement cafés. The bomb site is flooded to form an open air lido, with a picturesque backdrop of mid-Victorian façades which previously fronted the street (Fig. 1.7).

A model and plans for a new centre, in the post-war picturesque modern style, are enthusiastically adopted. Even the barbed wire cordon is literally undermined, as lads crawl under it to experience the rest of London as a foreign territory. They visit and enjoy London's monuments as if they are tourists, and escape back into the haven of Pimlico, newly defined by its imposed borders as different.

Like *Passport to Pimlico*, *It Happened Here* is a story of a fictional post-war era. But instead of winning, Britain has capitulated. A Nazi administration is established. The story is of a woman caught in the crossfire between Nazis and Allied Resistance. Following the shooting of her neighbours, she is forcibly evacuated from her west country village. In London she joins 'Immediate Action', a quasi-military, Fascist nursing corps. She is punished for helping a wounded partisan, and ends up at a tranquil country hospital unknowingly giving lethal injections to those no longer desired by the state. She escapes – the film ends with her capture by partisans.

The continuing preoccupation with the delineation of nationality is introduced in *It Happened Here*'s opening sequence. It uses an image familiar to Britons from another opening sequence: that of *Dad's Army*, a cosily nostalgic television comedy set in the early 1940s.[24] The Nazi onslaught through Europe is depicted as a series of invading arrows. In *Dad's Army*, however, plucky little arrows fend off the big European bully, and the sharp, white cliff edge to Britain remains intact. This defined island image is found again in the Ernö Goldfinger version of Abercrombie's Plan for London for the general public,[25] drawn up during the war. It introduced the idea of the Green Belt, a cordon of open land restraining London, beyond which new satellite towns could contain growth. The Goldfinger version depicts the growth of London as an uncontainable red peril spreading over the South East (see Chapter 6, Fig. 6.1). It has a plethora of images concerned with the need to contain, delineate and categorise (zone) urban activity. The cover actually shows *London* as an island like Britain, its edge defined by white cliffs (Fig. 1.8), whereas in the opening sequence of *It Happened Here* Britain is shown joined seamlessly with continental Europe. The

1.7 *Passport to Pimlico* (1948): Pimlico Lido.

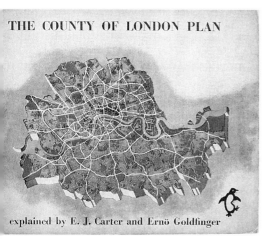

**1.8** *The County of London Plan* (1945) explained by E.J. Carter and Ernö Goldfinger: Front cover.

**1.9** *It Happened Here* (1956–63): Opening sequence.

arrows of Nazi progress overrun everywhere (Fig. 1.9). The film's ceaselessly chilling effect starts with an attack on the most familiar way the British defend the borders of their idea of nationhood: as an island.

*It Happened Here* describes a 'what if . . .?' London through icons of the capital's familiar normality as does *Passport to Pimlico*. Where *Passport* makes a point of featuring the No. 24 bus which continues to go to Pimlico, in *It Happened Here* the 159 red double-decker also carries on going to Streatham Common. It still advertises the *Picture Post*, but now it carries SS officers. Virtually every major physical symbol of stability is shown in occupation by Nazis; and each image delivers its own well-aimed punch in the groin of national self-knowledge. Nazis march outside the most famous survivor of the Blitz, the massive bombardment of London by Germany in 1940, St Paul's Cathedral. Nazified newspaper advertisements for familiar papers are displayed against the backdrop of the Mother of Parliaments (Fig. 1.10).

Nazi soldiers pay homage at the Albert Memorial, the monument erected by a grieving Queen Victoria to her dead German husband, provoking its insidious re-reading as a Teutonic Valhalla.

Brownlow and Mollo build up a palette of harsh contrasts: in each frame the two symbols of apparent categorical difference, British nationhood and Nazi supremacy, are clashed brutally together. What is depicted *within the film* is not, unlike the fantasy 1948 *Pimlico*, a set of transgressions, rule breakings and indeterminate hybrids: in *It Happened Here* two monoliths are shown in unassailable integrity, and the story is of an isolated individual caught between the two. What is under attack,

**1.10** *It Happened Here* (1956–63): Nazi images on newspaper advertisements outside the Houses of Parliament.

however, by the film *as a whole* is the same post-war fuzziness of position that Reyner Banham finds reprehensible in J.M. Richards. In architectural terms that can be understood as the view that the established, traditional built fabric of Britain is somehow inherently decent and reflective of national virtue. As it were in response, Brownlow and Mollo single out the unexceptional banality of the suburban terrace, the location of J.M. Richards' sense of nationhood, to site their most inescapably shocking episodes. It is the point where architectural and environmental iconography are apparently at their most cosy that the viewer searches in vain for respite from the film's remorseless violence. It is from the suburban terrace that the 'heroine' takes her measured decision to join the Fascist medical corps. It is in the Home Counties country house that she administers her lethal injections.

Both the content and the aesthetic of this New Wave film have a kinship with Brutalist preoccupations. Architecture was not alone among the arts in perceiving a feeble lack of direction in the post-war decade, characterised by the 1951 Festival of Britain. In 1956 the first Angry Young Man appears in the theatre, in synchrony with the completion of Hunstanton School: Banham notes that the 'revolt' of the younger generation of architects 'has been compared to the Angry Young Men of the British theatre'.[26] Jimmy Porter, John Osborne's protagonist in *Look Back in Anger* is not nice, he is brutal: to his wife he says: 'I want to see you grovel. I want to see your face rubbed in the mud.'[27] This contemporary description of the Angry Young Man is taken from Robert Hewison's book *In Anger*:

> A new hero has risen among us. He is consciously, even conscientiously, graceless. His face when not dead pan is set in a snarl of exasperation. He has one skin too few . . . it is the phoney to which his nerve endings are tremblingly exposed. At the least suspicion of the phoney he gets tough.[28]

It reads almost as a formal prescription of the soon-to-be popularised Brutalist style in architecture. The *moral* obligation of gracelessness is suggested by the word *conscientious*; 'his dead pan face', the façade of buildings which reject decorative false fronts; his 'one skin too few', the exposure of vital structure to the exterior without a mediating cover. And, above all, the assumption of honesty behind the driving rejection of the false and the phoney.

In 1959 the director Tony Richardson wrote:

> It is absolutely vital to get into British films the same sort of impact and sense of life that what you can loosely call the Angry Young Man cult has had in the theatre and literary worlds . . . It is a desperate need.[29]

Like Brutalism, the New Wave can be said to have had self-consciously avant-garde origins, manifested first in the magazine *Sequence*, founded in Oxford in 1947, and then in 1956 in the magazine *Free Cinema*, which 'set out to celebrate "the significance of the everyday" . . . The impetus was directly social.'[30] In *Free Cinema No. 1* Lindsay Anderson wrote:

> An attitude means a style. A style means an attitude. Implicit in our attitude is a belief in freedom, in the importance of people and the significance of the everyday.[31]

Robert Hewison comments that the cinema of the post-war years was 'still obstinately class bound; still rejecting the stimulus of contemporary life'.[32] In contrast, a contemporary commentator observed New Wave films confronted 'life as grey, grimy and desperately restricted, never more so than in its pleasures which are taken solemnly, and almost always end in quarrels'.[33] In similar spirit, Nigel Henderson, a member of the Independent Group's Brutalist core, exhibited black and white photographs of the East End at the 1953 ICA show *Parallel of Life and Art* which stressed the unsanitised reality of everyday life: Peter Smithson's defence of Brutalism through the categorical rhetoric of objectivity and truth, quoted above, echoes Anderson.

It is the automatic connection – still accepted without explanation – made in both Brutalist architecture and in filmic New Wave, between brutal, raw, uncovered aesthetic characteristics, and an intention of moral exposure that is remarkable.

The aesthetic affinity of the two media, Brutalist architecture and New Wave cinema, emerges in their mutual preoccupation with monochrome. While the black and white of *It Happened Here* was necessitated by its exceptionally cheap production costs, the mainstream films of the New Wave era – *A Taste of Honey, This Sporting Life, Saturday Night and Sunday Morning*[34] – arguably rejected well-developed colour technology. It was a move akin to Brutalism's own rejection of new, highly coloured, hybrid and artificial building materials, such as the plastic-based panelling, available by the early 1950s, and extensively used in the Festival of Britain. The devastating close-close-ups of *It Happened Here* introduce a sense of monochromatic texture absent from *Passport to Pimlico*. The nearest *Passport to Pimlico* gets to a close-up is a decorous composition of two or three people, or a protagonist talking to others – a technique which emphasises communality, not isolation. In the opening scenes of *It Happened Here* the camera pans across a wall (Fig. 1.11) in a set of frames demonstrating texture alone, to convey the flight of innocent people caught in crossfire between partisans and Nazis. The occupation of the whole frame with the shrapnelled face of a victim becomes a revelation of brutalised surface (Fig. 1.12).

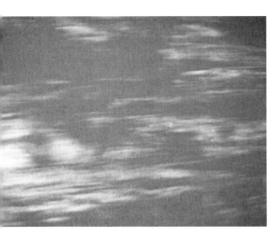

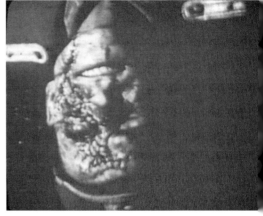

**1.11** *It Happened Here* (1956–63): Part of a 5-second sequence where the camera pans close up along a wall, revealing texture alone.

**1.12** *It Happened Here* (1956–63): Close-up of a shrapnelled face; deliberately upside down it focuses on its brutalised surface.

Brutalism's continuing sway over the prevailing architectural aesthetic is systematically revealed in the obsessional working of the monochrome building surface represented in *Rendering with Pen and Ink*.[35] *Rendering with Pen and Ink* was a technical manual of the early 1970s, aimed at architectural draughtsmen. The book describes an exhaustive catalogue of techniques achievable in the depiction of buildings' exteriors (Fig. 1.13), all within the honest restrictions and categorisations of the Brutalist palette. It is the raw surface of the actual material of construction, rather than any applied finish which is depicted.

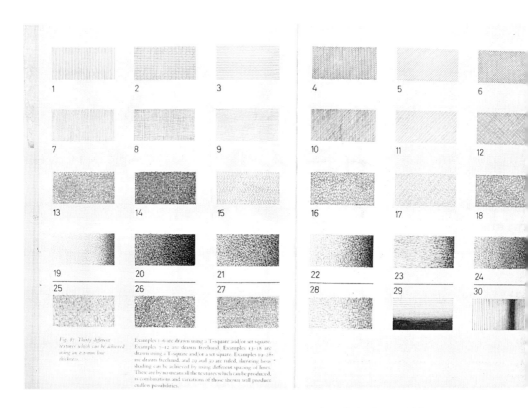

**1.13** *The Thames and Hudson Manual of Rendering with Pen and Ink* (1973): Catalogue of different surfaces available to the draughtsman using a consistent width of technical pen.

As in Brownlow and Mollo's film, variation is restricted and contained to shades of grey. This is compounded by the discipline imposed by a single-line thickness of technical pen. Ink is unable to flow through such pens unless they are used at a consistent vertical angle, giving an 'objective', i.e. non-varying, line. As virtually all production and presentation information used the technical pen, mainstream office practice gave, by default, the capabilities of such a pen decisive authority over what could and could not be depicted. The book *Community Decay*[36] of the same period, presents the unpalatable reality of sub-standard housing-stock statistics using the same technique as *Rendering with Pen and Ink*.

Textured monochromatic block charts represent the extent of deprivation. These block charts have the form and textural quality of graphic representations of Brutalist-derived panel built tower blocks, constructed to replace the outdated terraced house (Fig. 1.14). An image from the book juxtaposes just such a terraced house from an inner London suburb, with a page of unassailable 'truths' representing the raw horror of what lurks, covered up, and undeclared within.

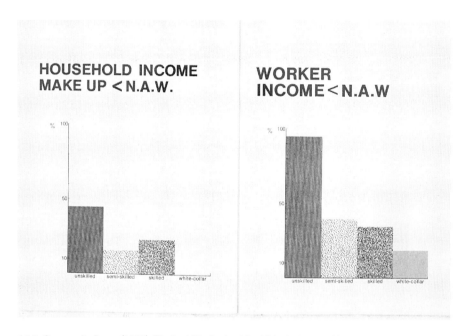

**1.14** *Community Decay* (1973): The brutal truth about the Victorian terraced houses.

This image of stark abutment of the apparently known and familiar with the revealed truth can be read against *It Happened Here*'s own image of a terraced house with a row of armed Nazis stationed in front.

Both images attack the deceptive harmlessness of accepted signifiers of normality and Britishness. Both the image from *Community Decay* and from *It Happened Here* seek to demonstrate unarguably that just 'here' is where it can, and does, 'happen'.

The Brutalist champion and the New Wave film-maker loathe moral and social ambiguity, sentimentality (a key term of condemnation in Reyner Banham's writing), and fuzziness. It follows that these aesthetics challenge the sentimentality and ambiguity of cultural symbols in general. In particular, they challenge the belief that *architectural* symbols whether the monument (St Paul's/Skylon), or the suburban family home (*The Castles on the Ground*) can convey a consistent and good meaning. As we have seen, *It Happened Here* methodically gathers up the major architectural symbols of London's fight for democracy and freedom, and cancels them out by the unequivocally brutal presence of the Nazis. The brutal technique is needed to cut through a decade or more of myth-making and propaganda, during war-time and after, which relied on unspoken and unclarified association. The earlier film, *Passport to Pimlico*, deliberately plays with notions of fuzziness, challenging restriction and categorisation, but this is played out against the stability of defined certainties. Britishness, for example, is symbolised by the dilapidated but unconquered fabric of London. As in J.M. Richards' book *The Castles on the Ground*, the notion that a benign nationhood resides mysteriously in the established architectural fabric is unchallenged. Brownlow and Mollo's film is in direct opposition to such an assumption: in Peter Smithson's words, it faces up, in a big way, to the reality of post-war life: it is concerned with dragging to the surface what we are in the habit of covering up.

The Brutalist demand for demonstrable honesty has an inevitable architectural result: inside becomes the same as outside. The Smithson's Hunstanton School is the archetypal example of this. The constructional system of panel and frame requires that both panel and frame are visible from both sides of the wall, inside and outside (Fig. 1.2) and (Fig. 1.3). Anything less would entail a covering up, an obscuring of the self-evident truth of the construction. Moreover, it is essential for the maintenance of purity that the distinct element, the wall, is unsmeared at the edges, and is seen to be clearly delineated. In this way, the interior, separate and distinct from the outside, begins to be called into question.

*Beat Girl* (1960, directed by Edmond T. Greville) takes up this architectural theme. 'A risible expose-style melodrama' according to *Halliwell's Film Guide*,[37] the protagonists are a successful architect, his new young wife, and his teenage daughter. The film is a prurient B-feature showing a young girl taking to drugs, drink and sex. It draws a parallel with the architect's denial of the physical interior of their domestic home, and his synonymous denial and ignorance of his daughter's *interior* life – what is going on in her head. To express this, the film creates a unique inside architecture. While it presents a surface Brutalism of raw concrete panelling, the filmic interior makes explicit all that is denied by such an aesthetic – i.e. the messy trappings of everyday life – by situating them *within the interior of the wall itself* (Figs 1.15 and 1.16).

**1.15** *Beat Girl* (1960): The TV lurks behind its concrete screen.

To make this dramatic point, the film creates the impossible: a Brutalist interior which, far from being merely the other side of the wall, is a manifestly deliberate insert. It is situated within the conventional brick-built exterior of a suburban house with the usual trappings, including decorative awning and window boxes. The opening scenes of *Beat Girl* show a Rolls-Royce drawing up to this London house, containing architect and new bride. Once inside, the double-skinned wall, like an exceptionally narrow haunted house, reveals to the viewer the hidden world which its austere surface forbids. The interior is wholly lined with concrete panelling: it is a Brutalist hybrid. To compound the irony, all the accoutrements of a conventional pre-war life, against which the spirit of Brutalism railed, are present and correct. So the hall, complete with its concrete panelled stair, is the meeting place for the immaculately uniformed elderly housekeeper to greet the young bride (Fig. 1.17).

The conventions slip effortlessly into this new aesthetic austerity. And as effectively as if tucked behind a pre-war green baize door, the new interior has done away not just with the signs of domesticity, but with all signs of human inhabitation.

**1.16** *Beat Girl* (1960): The wall contains Beat Girl's messy record collection.

**1.17** *Beat Girl* (1960): Housekeeper greets architect and new bride in concrete panelled  hallway.

The contemporary diagrams from *Parker Morris*[38] (Fig. 1.18), the most influential of government documents governing new standards in housing, graphically demonstrate the assumption of inside-as-outside. The diagrams indicate that the interior, conceived as a separate, individual realm with uniquely personal household goods, no longer applies. The logic of inside-as-outside requires that the objects inhabiting the interior must be both *similar* to those of the exterior and *transparent from* the exterior.

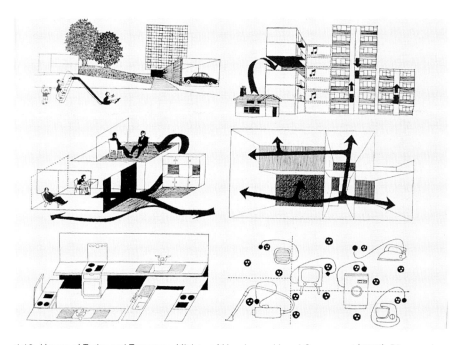

**1.18** *Homes of Today and Tomorrow, Ministry of Housing and Local Government* (1963): Diagrams by Gordon Cullen.

The objects in the diagram are standard, mass produced, both predicted and prescribed. There is consequently no possibility for the inclusion of the impure, the hybrid, and the uncategorised. The enclosure serves the clearly defined and exposed commodities of your interior life, which must be standardised to 'go with' your home: the unexpected, unpredictable, domestic object is excluded.

The contemporary acceptance of this mind-set is widespread. It is revealed when Ronan Point, a system-built tower block in the East End of London, collapsed in May 1968, killing four people (Fig. 1.19). As might be expected, the collapse heralded an unseemly scrambling among building professionals to assign blame to

**1.19** *Architects' Journal* (1968):
Close-up of the collapse of Ronan Point
tower block, Newham, London.

anyone but themselves. The final leader in the *Architects' Journal* of that year,[39]
declares 'gas is far and away the most dangerous (cause of explosions) as regards the
likelihood of structural damage' and concludes 'why not ban gas?'. An earlier letter
from Sam Webb[40] points out that if gas is cut off and the block becomes all electric,
'The tenants will, almost without exception, resort to paraffin and store 5 gallon
drums to top up their heater'; and he notes that when the constructional joints were
tested, they had failed at the equivalent explosion to just two pints of petrol in a room.
Thus, the heaters, which do not fit into the predicted catalogue, are by default classed
as trespassing hybrids, and blamed for the disaster. That the architect failed to sort
out a system of enclosure flexible enough to accommodate the unpredictable
messiness of life, without risking death to the tenants, is an explanation that does not
appear to have been considered.

In *Beat Girl* such transgressive, messy, unclassified objects appear polemically
within the wall which at Ronan Point, fatally, refuses their presence. The excluded
objects of the Beat Girl's individuality: the record player, the television, disappear
behind sliding concrete panels, which, when closed, return the wall to its *apparently*

**1.20** Sitting room at Half Hyde, Shepall, Stevenage, UK (1957).

*honest* state. The wall dictates the conditions of everyday life. In contrast, an interior at Stevenage New Town (Fig. 1.20), exhibits the domestic character of a typical picturesque-style modern house.

The room divider is a wall exclusively designed for the interior, with no structural purpose. Where the signs of personality, and of a separate domestic realm in the Beat Girl's life are suppressed, here such objects as the TV, books and ornaments, are both displayed and celebrated. It is a pre-Brutalist interior, where the collecting of disparate, uncategorisable objects is admitted and enjoyed. The image from Stevenage can be read in the context of a pre-Brutalist relationship between inside and outside, one which espouses the picturesque and eschews dictatorship by the wall. J.M. Richards' contemporary and proprietor at the *Architectural Review*, Hugh de Cronin Hastings, defines such a compositional aesthetic of inclusion in his 1949 article *Townscape: a plea for an English Visual Philosophy.*[41]

> Nine people out of ten are surrounded in the home by household goods whose arrangement is as capricious as their origin is various: a Biedermeier escritoire, a horsehair chair covered in chintz, an Aalto table, or a less arty assortment from Great Aunts, the Near East and Oxford Street . . . yet the taste can be extremely high that quite ordinary

tasteless philistines show in the disposition and relationship of their bits and pieces even when those pieces are intrinsically worthless. There are thousands of homes of families-in-the-street which can offer satisfying arrangements of objects simply because their owners pursue unselfconsciously the Picturesque philosophy of giving every object the best possible chance to be itself.

In the Stevenage interior, the trappings of conventional life are incorporated into a modern aesthetic; conversely, the technology of the new is subordinated to notions such as cosy corners taken from the old. It is a hybrid.

The film's cautionary tale of the interior extends to the Beat Girl herself. The domestic interior explicitly requires that she herself is treated like an object: her individuality is unaccommodated and unrecognised. If the Picturesque philosophy gives every object the best possible chance to be itself, de Cronin Hastings is describing the chance the Beat Girl has been denied. Her unnaturally tidy room, with its meticulously categorised clothes hidden in the built-in wardrobe, is an environment wholly unreceptive to her tears of isolation.

The argument of this chapter has been that within both architecture and culture at large the covering up which Brutalism and the New Wave attack is both literal and symbolic. *It Happened Here* is concerned with the way things *are*. The aesthetic is accomplished: and the camera loves both its brutal subject and its brutal technique. Like the theatre's Angry Young Man, the medium of film itself allows a simultaneity: it is possible both to cry out against the way things are, to depict them in their horror, and at the same time to establish an ultimately acceptable new aesthetic which has as its benchmark raw honesty. Even taking into account that commercial considerations and public taste may demand a less remorseless art form of cinema and theatre, the comparison of architecture and film in this period of Britain's life reveals a fundamental problem. For an *architecture*, rather than a form like film, to commit itself to a remorseless depiction of the way things *are* rather than the way things *should be* is a profoundly radical departure from the utopian aspirations that lie behind the very act of building. At the smallest scale building involves transformation, and some investment in the future. This possibility the Brutalist aesthetic denies. The consistent revulsion of the non-architectural public for Brutalism, to whose lives it specifically addressed itself, can, and should, be reconsidered within this context. The inhabitants of new Brutalist public housing were afforded an Angry Young Architecture: a solidified ironic commentary on how things are, to the exclusion of the expression of future hope for the way things could be. The Beat Girl's own inability to occupy the territory of her own home signposts the inevitable schism between these two projects: the brutally honest depiction of the way things are, and the way things should, or could be.

## Notes

1    Contemporary commentators – for example, the 'New Empiricism' edition of the Architectural Review – acknowledged the hybrid styles debt to Swedish modernism. The argument here is that this so-called 'empirical' modernism was adopted because it was understood within an already estsablished picturesque tradition.

2    '. . . "the British New Wave". The phrase was coined in echo of the French nouvelle vogue of distinctive films of around the same time to refer to what was seen as an analogous breakthrough in the production of British film.' Arthur Marwick, *The Sixties*, (UK: Oxford University Press, 1998), pp. 117–18.

3    Mary Douglas, *Purity and Danger: An Analysis of the Concepts of Pollution and Taboo*, (London: Routledge, 1966), p. 122.

4    Reyner Banham, *The New Brutalism*, (London: The Architectural Press, 1966).

5    Ibid., p. 12.

6    Ibid., p. 13.

7    Ibid., p. 17.

8    Alison and Peter Smithson, *Architectural Design*, (London, April 1957), p. 14.

9    See discussion under the sub-heading 'Structural Truth' in this book's *Endpiece*.

10   Banham, op. cit., p. 13.

11   J.M. Richards, *The Castles on the Ground*, (London: The Architectural Press, 1946).

12   Banham, op. cit., p. 13.

13   Richards, op. cit., p. 14.

14   Ibid., p. 15.

15   Ibid., p. 18.

16   Ibid., pp. 55–6.

17   Acronym for the International Congresses for Modern Architecture, founded in 1928 by a group of leading modern architects.

18   Joan Ockman, editor, *Architecture Culture 1943–1968*, (New York: Columbia Books on Architecture/Rizzoli, 1993), p. 100.

19   Acronym for Modern Architectural Research Group, British wing of CIAM founded in 1932.

20   Anne Massey in her book *The Independent Group – Modernism and Mass Culture in Britain 1945–1959*, (Manchester and New York: Manchester University Press, 1995), notes the interest in truth was more than rhetorical for the progenitors of Brutalism. 'Their second session consisted of a talk by Alfred Jules Ayer, the most prominent British exponent of the philosophy of logical positivism . . . In his complete rejection of all metaphysical statements as unverifiable by experience, Ayer provided the Group with a valuable philosophical framework for defining its position' (p. 48).

21   Ockman, op. cit., p. 121.

22    Ockman, op. cit., p. 120.

23    Mary Banham and Bevis Hillier, editors, *A Tonic to the Nation: The Festival of Britain 1951*, (London: Thames & Hudson, 1976), p. 45.

24    *It Happened Here* predates *Dad's Army* by a number of years.

25    *The County of London Plan explained by E.J. Carter and Ernö Goldfinger*, (London: Penguin, 1945).

26    Banham, op. cit., p. 13.

27    Quoted from *Look Back in Anger*, in Anthony Aldgate, *Censorship and the Permissive Society – British Cinema and Theatre 1955–1965*, (Oxford: Clarendon Press, 1995), p. 76.

28    Walter Allen writing in *The New Statesman*, quoted in Robert Hewison, *In Anger: British Culture in the Cold War 1945–60*, (New York: Oxford University Press, 1981), p. 116.

29    Quoted in Aldgate, op. cit., p. 74.

30    Penelope Houston, *The Contemporary Cinema*, (London: Penguin, 1963), p. 114.

31    Quoted in Hewison, op. cit., p. 153.

32    Ibid.

33    Penelope Houston, op. cit., p. 118.

34    *A Taste of Honey* (UK: British Lion, 1961), director: Tony Richardson, *This Sporting Life* (UK: Rank/Independent Artists, 1963), director: Lindsay Anderson, *Saturday Night and Sunday Morning* (UK: Bryanston/Woodfall, 1960), director: Karel Reisz. These three New Wave films are typically set, unlike *It Happened Here*, in the North of England, an accepted cultural signifier of authenticity, and life in the raw.

35    Robert W. Gill, *The Thames and Hudson Manual of Rendering with Pen and Ink*, (London: Thames & Hudson, 1973).

36    Jon Rowland, *Community Decay*, (London: Penguin, 1973).

37    Leslie Halliwell (edited by John Walker), *Halliwell's Film Guide*, (London: HarperCollins, 1994).

38    Ministry of Housing and Local Government, *Homes for Today & Tomorrow*, (London, Her Majesty's Stationery Office, 1961).

39    *Architects' Journal*, (London, 20 November 1968) p. 1172.

40    *Architects' Journal*, (London, 4 September 1968) p. 429.

41    Quoted in Ockman, op. cit., p. 115.

# Chapter 2
## Why does your flat leak?

**2.1** Private housing estate, Docklands, London, UK (1992).

This is a chapter about building construction. The sharp end of the public disaffection with Britain's period of mass reconstruction in the 1960s is the straightforward, technical failure of its housing. It leaks. The scale of Britain's rebuilding means we will continue to pay the economic price of these buildings' failure well into the future. Huge amounts of literature have been devoted to accounting for this failure. They situate it, in the main, in a technical context – poor supervision, cost-cutting, inappropriate components.

Here though, is another unanswered question, one most frequently on the lips of the inhabitants of the vast housing estates riddled with defects. Did architects *know* they were building an architecture which literally *could not hold water*? Is it possible, in other words, that there was a mind-set which made the profession perceive other issues as more pressing and more crucial than water penetration?

This chapter questions the assumption that architectural beliefs have had no role in validating building construction. It is in the face of the overwhelming unpopularity of post-war buildings that architects have claimed that the fact that too many buildings leak has nothing to do with them. But in its reconstruction of post-war Britain under the Welfare State, the building industry used the provision of public housing as an expansive experimental playground. Never, in fact, had so much been architect designed, for clients with so silent a voice.

Of all the issues dealt with in this book, this is the one that has most bearing on the livelihood of architects, and the profit margins of the building industry. And so, to put it crudely, this is the question that will be most veiled by habits that need to seem natural, rational and sensible – and so apparently pointless to probe. In fact, when Marx called 'ideology' the set of ideas that prevent the vested interests of our rulers from being examined, he might have had building construction in mind. The final part of this chapter looks at two allegorical fictions, architectural installations and accompanying writings, constructed with the specific intent of unravelling these assumptions about how and why we build the way we do.

As in Chapter 1, the analysis of the origins of taboos against pollution by Mary Douglas provides identifying characteristics allowing me to speculate on a link between different representations of building construction. To recap: this concerns the idea of *the defence of the border*. Borders hold in what is defined and pure. These characteristics allows identification of the pure in contrast to the hybrid: the pure can have a line drawn clearly round it; the pure can be reduced to an original set of classes; the borders between the *form* of the pure and the *formlessness* outside it, are well defined and self-evident.

There is another characteristic which idenitifies the pure establishing itself in opposition to the dirty, and undelineated, that is particularly pertinent to building construction. And that is defence of the border through *classification*. In natural science, classification requires the identification of particular characteristics allowing you to say unequivocally that the specimen is this class of butterfly, that class of ant. Borders are therefore more firmly fixed the more distinct, and separate, the definition of classes. It follows that the more effectively the border is defended, the more classification expands. In this chapter, I argue that the ceaseless growth of specialist building components depends on the tendency to expand categories of classification, in combination with the economic needs of the industry to keep increasing its markets. In this light, the genesis of the cavity wall in Britain, a banal double-skinned brick exterior (Fig. 2.1), enclosing state-of the art technology within its own narrow interior, is but the most recent stage in the battle of the border, rather than a triumph of modern building science.

To start, though, I look at the *forms* of presentation of building construction, both now and in the 1960s, as so many unacknowledged professional fictions. I look at *how* building construction presents itself more than the technical intricacies of what it appears to be saying. Building construction's forms of self-presentation include the Common Sense and the Practical, Science and Classification, Tolerance, Structural Honesty and the Traditional. As in some examinations of fiction, this inquiry involves close reading of the descriptive texts of building construction, which can seem very minute. So some patience is needed to follow the arguments from this detailed, apparently particular examples to the general points.

## The common sense and the practical

In construction, as in car maintenance, common sense prevents your asking 'Why'; the practical leaves you endlessly trying to find out 'How'. Books on construction are often presented in the form of a handbook, as something that is practically useful, like a guide to motor mechanics.

**2.2** *GLC Good Practice Details* (1979): Front cover.

**2.3** Front cover, car maintenance manual.

Perhaps it goes without saying that this format is intended to appeal to men, for the same information could equally be well conveyed in the same format as *Elle* magazine menu cards. A paradigmatic example of this approach for the current generation of British architects is the Greater London Council's GLC *Good Practice*

*Details* (1979) (Fig. 2.2).[1] When the Greater London Council replaced the London County Council in the 1960s, it took over the largest architects department in the world.[2] This was the heyday of post-war reconstruction, a time when the number of new dwellings built topped 400,000 a year. The LCC had been responsible for much of the innovation in construction techniques, particularly in system building, where the components are manufactured in factories off site.[3] However, the publication of the GLC's good practice and standard details handbooks coincided with, arguably, the high point of public outcry against modern architects and architecture. The books' bland, matter-of-fact style is singularly effective in eradicating controversy and loss of faith – the presentation in the style of a practical manual makes the search for belief systems seem absurd. As in the drawing handbook *Rendering in Pen and Ink*[4] of the same period, details are drawn 'mechanically', that is with technical pen, a method which makes the body imitate the predictable movements of the machine, requiring a constant line and the use of a straight edge (Fig. 2.4).

Handwriting is eliminated in favour of the stencil, and with it, any notion that future circumstances might call for changes, adaptation or amendment. There is no reference to when or where these details were actually built: they are ahistorical, incontrovertibly valid for all time.

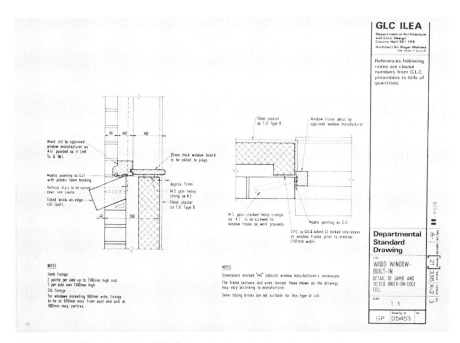

**2.4** *GLC Good Practice Details* (1979): Drawing of section through cavity wall.

The GLC belongs to an era of modernist certainties now past. But the practical common-sense approach to construction prevails: it successfully adapts itself to the post-modern world. Cecil Handisyde's construction guide of 1976, popular for its comforting title, *Everyday Details*,[5] adopts a relativist and pluralist approach to the apparent certainties of cavity wall construction (Fig. 2.5). Each chapter of the book presents several possible versions of a single detail (Fig. 2.6). The drawings are specifically produced in a robust, workaday manner; they are freehand, and notes appear in the guise of amendable – and controvertible – handwriting.

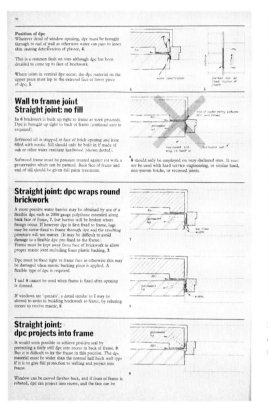

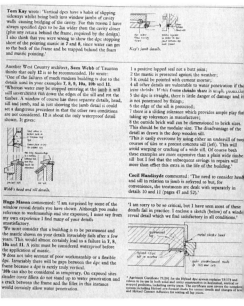

**2.6** *Everyday Details* (1976): Minute variations in a dispute over the configuration of the cavity wall: more jamb details.

**2.5** *Everyday Details* (1976): Minute variations in a dispute over the configuration of the cavity wall: jamb details.

The details were first published in the *Architects' Journal*, a weekly magazine aimed at the profession. Some of the different versions have emanated from readers who have written in to take issue with the published detail. This is a dialectical approach to building construction involving wise old practitioners battling out on the pages of a book. Here they are discussing in minute detail how to avoid water penetration in a cavity wall:

> Plymouth architect, Michael Boulesteix, objected to stopping the vertical dpc flush with the brickwork and insisted that it should be taken into the cavity: 'It is standard practice in this office to project vertical damp-proof courses at least 4 in. into the cavity beyond the closing walls as shown on the attached sketches. We have learned from bitter experience that the usual method of stopping the dpc at the same width as the closing inner leaf is totally inadequate in the conditions of severe exposure we have to design for in the West Country' . . . Cecil Handisyde commented: 'This is a good point and one also made in the next letter by London architect, Tom Kay of Tom Kay Associates, although I question the practicability of Kay's second point.' Tom Kay wrote: '. . . I also think that you were wrong to show the dpc stopping short of the pointing mastic in 7 and 8, since the water can get back into the frame and be trapped behind the foam and mastic pointing' (included in this book's Fig. 2.5). Another West Country architect, Sam Webb of Taunton . . . wrote: 'One of the failures of much modern building is due to the details used in your examples . . . Whereas water may be stopped from entering at the jamb it will still nevertheless run down the edges of the sill and rot the timber' . . . Handisyde commented: 'The need to consider head and sill in relation to jamb is referred to but, for convenience, the treatments are dealt with separately . . . ' Hugo Mason commented: 'I am surprised by some of the window reveal details you have shown . . . 9 (included in this book's Fig. 2.5) does not take account of poor workmanship or a flexible dpc . . . I am sorry to be so critical, but I have seen most of these details fail in practice.'[6]

But in fact these battles are not at all liberal, or relativist. They are like medieval disputes over the number of angels who could dance on the head of a pin. All argument is in relation to a given detail, already published by Handisyde, drawn in section or plan and at a scale of 1:5. So disagreement is confined to the reconfiguration of a given set of elements. The lines or edges of the accepted components of architecture therefore remain intact: they are successfully defended. The terms of the dispute are set, and any alternative approach requiring a minute adjustment, or a large-scale spatial change, or a move that cannot be described using a line or a standard orthographic drawing, plan or section, is proscribed from the outset. All the disputers take for granted either that the addition of new specialist components, or the reconfiguration of existing ones, will ultimately provide the desired result.

Handisyde's characterisation of construction as a series of Problems – reflected in his chapter titles: 'Masonry walls: dpc at base of external walls'; 'External doors:

position of frame', etc. – means that details inevitably constitute Solutions. The Practical and the Common Sense fix a set of delineated elements that you have to deal with. In the world of construction, it is impossible to say 'I wouldn't have started with that premise in the first place.'

## Science and classification

Post-war building construction has a dream of science as an ordering, purifying system. This dream is graphically illustrated in this prediction for the building site of the future, made in 1967 by the RIBA technical adviser:

> A group of almost white-coated, well-paid workers, slotting and clipping standard components into place in rhythmic sequence on an orderly, networked and mechanised site, to a faultless programme, without mud, mess, sweat or swearing.[7]

No dirt will be allowed to get out of place: that much is clear. But such clean ordering depends on the clear delineation of the constructional elements: they must be clipped and slotted, their edges free of the distorting smears of mud or mess. If science requires ever greater classification and differentiation of its constituent parts, then progress in building construction – a self-styled science – emulates this. Any perception of a new 'problem' is an opportunity, not just for a new dispute about the choreography of the parts of construction for practitioners, but, for the building industry, a new component. The expanding reams of product literature the industry produces – itself to be ordered and filed – present column after column of specialist, unadaptable building components.

The use of a metric numbering system (as in Fig. 2.7) to identify the parts of a technical information sheet had been widely adopted in Britain by the end of the 1960s. It reflected (a) a concern to define classes; (b) the need to present architectural practice, and the process of specification as practical; and (c) the presentation of a limited set of constructional alternatives as universal. It was paralleled by a mania for modularising all building components.

Absolutism was the state of mind of the contemporary guardians of technical objectivity. This is nowhere better indicated than in the 1969 *Architects' Journal* Technical Sheet entitled 'Joints and Jointing'. With the certainty of an 18th-century encyclopaedist, the anonymous author declares that:

> there is no such thing as a traditional, modern or industrialised building, only a difference of the constituent parts, with different scales: and jointing techniques.[8]

| Product | Function | Applications | Sizes | Colours | Standard Package | Suitability Equivalent | Page No. in Brochure 2 |
|---|---|---|---|---|---|---|---|
| Type W | Cavity wall perp vent/weep | New and existing work. Dual-function product ventilates and weeps. Insect, water and air baffles | 105/115 x 65 x 10mm plus lock lid wedges | Grey, black, beige, brown, terracotta, white | Boxes of 50 | 390mm² | 20 |
| Type W Extension | Connects into Type W to form king-size through-vent | Increased length ideal for venting through cavity walls, under floors, roof areas and confined spaces | 200/225 x 65 x 10mm | Grey | Boxes of 50 | 390mm² | 20 |
| Airbrick | Brick-format ventilation, with external grill, internal water check and wind baffles | Most cavity/room/under floor ventilation applications | 220 x 60 x 70mm | Terracotta, beige, slate | Boxes of 20 | 6600mm² | 4 |
| Airbricks | Brick-format ventilation, with external grill, internal water check and wind baffles | All brick ventilators can be clipped together as illustrated, thus all permutations of size available from one standard brick | 220 x 60 x 70mm | Terracotta, beige, slate | Boxes of 20 | 6600mm² 13200mm² 19800mm² | 4 |
| Straight Sleeve | Connects to airbrick to provide duct sleeve across cavity. Supplied with DPC cavitray | Conveys airbrick intake to inside skin, essential if cavity fill is incorporated | Approximately 224 x 74 x 300mm | Black/natural | Boxes of 10 | 6600mm² 13200mm² 19800mm² | 6 |
| Cranked Sleeve | Accepts standard airbrick Adjustable telescopic height | Under floor ventilation | Standard brick fitting with 2 brick, 3 brick and 4 brick height alternatives | Black | Boxes of 10 | 6600mm² | 6 |
| Cranked Sleeve Extension | Permits cranked sleeve to be extended to greater depth difference | Under floor ventilation | Approximately 225 x 50 x 450mm | Black | Boxes of 10 | 6600mm² | 6 |
| Room Vent Pack No 1 | Airbrick, telescopic sleeve and interior grill kit | Provides designed ventilation to habitable room. New work | Single brick size satisfies habitable room background ventilation requirements | Brick – terracotta Sleeve – black Grill – white | Single set | 3097mm² | 16 |
| Gas Appliance Pack No 1 | Airbrick, telescopic sleeve and interior grill (walls) | Provides designed ventilation for room in which a gas appliance is sited (select packs/capacity to suit appliance) | One brick size pack provides airflow of 3,225mm² Normally suitable for up to 50,000BTU | Brick – terracotta Sleeve – black Grill – white | Single set | Appliance up to 50,000BTU | 16 |
| Gas Appliance Pack No 2 | Airbrick sleeve and interior grill (walls) | Provides designed ventilation for room in which a gas appliance is sited (select packs/capacity to suit appliance) | Double brick size pack provides airflow of 12,581mm² Normally suitable for up to 125,000BTU | Brick – terracotta Sleeve – black Grill – white | Single set | Appliance up to 125,000BTU | 16 |
| Type V | Eaves ventilator | New work, all pitches Type V incorporates integral fixings | Available to suit truss centres of 400, 450 or 600mm | Natural galvanized finish | Boxes of 10 | 10mm continuous gap | 19 |
| Type V with fly screen | Eaves ventilator | As standard V, but with fly screen making it suitable for open eaves applications, 15° upwards | Available to suit truss centres of 400, 450 or 600mm | Natural galvanized steel and PVC | Boxes of 10 | 10mm continuous gap | 19 |
| Type T | High performance ventilator 'clamps' trusses at any centres Suits all truss centres Suits all roof pitches | Universal eaves ventilator | Approximately 180 x 400 x 100mm | Black | Boxes of 25 | 25mm continuous gap | 18 |

51

**2.7** Cavity wall accessories.

Thus, all previous disputes on the history of styles are dismissed by paragraph 1.02 of a joint information package. In the context of construction, science's role is to render everything measurable, to attach a number to it, and to make sure each thing keeps to its assigned class.

## Tolerance

In 1968 the Beatles released the song *A Day in the Life*, on the album *Sergeant Pepper's Lonely Hearts Club Band*,[9] which includes the following lines:

> Ten thousand holes in Blackburn, Lancashire
> And though the holes were rather small
> They had to count them all
> Now they know how many holes it takes
> To fill the Albert Hall

The year before, the *Architects' Journal* published its Technical Sheet entitled 'Jointing Between Pre-Cast Concrete Facade Panels – Tolerances Achieved in Vertical Joints',[10] in which it was revealed that the Cement and Concrete Association had surveyed the widths of more than 4,300 joints made since 1964. The more a construction method is component based, and the more distinct and unadaptable its individual elements, the more tolerance, and a fear of failure leading to leaks, become a focus of concern. For it is at the point where most effort is made to defend the borders of a component, the junctions between the separate *forms* of absolutely defined parts, that a building is at its most vulnerable to that most *formless* of elements, water.

To tolerate is to 'endure, permit, forbear to judge harshly or rigorously . . . hence permissible variation in dimension'.[11] If you build in a tolerance in building construction, you are acknowledging that edges may not always be in the exact place where lines have officially been drawn. Tolerances become crucial when a component of construction does not tolerate – in the sense of *endure* or *permit* – other kinds of building construction. A *harsh* or *rigorous* form of construction cannot vary to allow the presence of other components. An example of this is panel construction. A pre-made panel arrives on site, intended to abut another already in place.

Just like a party: two people get into conversation, and it becomes clear that, come what may, each is going to maintain their opinions, and the one person cannot be affected in any way by the other. If you are the host this puts you under enormous strain. You have to accommodate both persons. You have to be almost infinitely flexible, capable of being pulled between one side and the other without snapping. In this way, someone whose role should be incidental, merely a means of introducing two others, becomes overwhelmingly decisive. In his role as a flexible mastic joint, the host is subjected to an intolerable level of stress trying to keep two panels together. He does the constructional equivalent of retiring to the kitchen and getting drunk (Fig. 2.8).

1 *Designers often have unrealistic expectations of mastic performance. The mastic sealant in joint to parapet below coping has suffered loss of adhesion and detachment; opening up between the mastic and the sides of the joint indicates the amount of movement.*

**2.8** Mastic failure between panels.

The very idea, basic to modern construction, that it is possible to establish a measurable, quantifiable dimension for tolerances seems questionable. The concept of tolerance is a central tenet of liberalism: hence the statement: 'I disagree with what you say, but I defend to the death your right to say it.' Within such a philosophy there can be no exceptions. It is no good saying, 'I can't endure you, as I've just spent 369 days putting up with another 369 like you' – that is intolerance – despite every one of the other 369 tolerant encounters. The *Architects' Journal* article claims that its survey demonstrates that only one in 370 joints will differ from the specified design width by more than the 'maximum tolerance'. But we know that the installation of just one panel outside the tolerance allowed will cause a leak. The mastic will tear, a hole will appear and water will get in. This leak will affect the whole building. It doesn't matter then that it is only one panel out of 370: in matters of tolerance, statistics are irrelevant, for tolerance by definition must be able to accommodate even the most extreme circumstances.

## Structural honesty

The previous chapter indicated how a belief in structural honesty means it is not enough to know that an arch rests on a column, or that this element supports that one: you have to *prove* that you are structurally honest: you have to *see* it to believe it. The resulting requirement that the building is visually transparently honest has direct consequences for its final appearance. Visual transparency requires the absolute delineation of the building's structural components. If there is any fuzziness or bastardisation between two parts, how will anyone know that you are being honest? This component must not be permitted to do that task, as then dangerous ambiguity is introduced. In useful tandem with the profit motives of an industrialised building industry, structural honesty in and of itself demands the specialisation of roles in building construction.

Hunstanton School (Figs. 1.2 and 1.3) does not leak. But its hugely influential constructional aesthetic, Brutalism, can be read as a prophetic litany of the types of building failure that have dogged British architecture, particularly public housing, since the 1960s and 1970s. Brickwork is treated as a panel that sits inside the structural frame. To be structurally honest it must be patently visible that this is so, from both the inside and the outside of the building. To achieve this, the Inside must merely be the Other Side of the wall, revealing the exact same conditions as the Outside.

This means that the frame may admit cold – unimpeded – from the outside to the inside. On the Inside, which, unlike the Outside, is heated, moisture in the air is condensed onto the cold frame, which then corrodes. The frame acts like a massive cold bridge from inside to outside. It exaggerates differential movement between panel and frame, which as we've seen is a direct consequence of their clear and honest differentiation as elements. If elements can move around like this, they will probably end up letting in water.

Looking round Britain you can see that the need to be honest about the presence of a structural slab has brought the puritanical chill of architectural ideology straight into the heart of innumerable people's own homes. In Westwood Piet and Partners' Moore Barracks at Shorncliffe, Kent (1969) the concrete slab of the floor is unambiguously visible, in contrast to the non-structural brickwork that forms the external wall (Fig. 2.9). It exemplifies a kind of construction familiar in public housing all over Britain.

The Moore Barracks were published as a building study, that is, as a technical exemplar, in the *Architects' Journal* (Fig. 2.10). The constructional details were praised for their structural honesty:

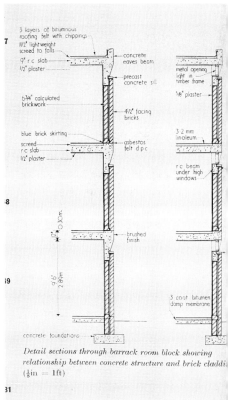

*Detail sections through barrack room block showing relationship between concrete structure and brick cladding ($\frac{1}{8}$in = 1ft)*

**2.9** Moore Barracks, Shorncliffe, Kent (1969): Westwood Piet & Partners.

**2.10** Moore Barracks (1969): Section through wall.

The external skin of brickwork is non structural. The continuous clerestory allows this to be expressed (i.e. seen) by sloping back the face of the stub columns. This logical structural device is also visually satisfying and gives a light hearted lift to the design.[12]

Given the prevailing Structurally Honest mind-set, this 'logical structural device' is employed to make the following points: (1) the concrete is structural i.e. it is holding the building up; (2) we can see this because it sits on another element of the structure, the inner face of the brickwork cavity wall; and (3) it rejects contact with potentially contaminating Non-Structure – the external brickwork skin – so it slopes its face, to make absolutely certain that we can see it is resting *behind* the external face of the brickwork and *on* the inner one. This building does not leak. However, we could imagine that, when it rains, water runs down that honest, sloping face of the concrete slab columns and, aided by capillary action, straight on to the inner skin of the cavity wall, which, though structural, is nevertheless inside and therefore might reasonably be expected to remain dry. Ideology (Structurally Honest Ideology, at any rate) is at odds with life without an umbrella.

## The traditional

The notion of structural honesty continues in use to legitimise the work of contemporary 'designer' architects such as Norman Foster. Despite this, public rejection of Brutalism and system-built modernism means that away from the architectural profession, structural honesty no longer figures in the portfolio of rationales used to justify the new wave of so-called 'traditional' housing construction that has been built, and continues to be built, by the private sector. Product literature from the building supply industry, on the other hand, reveals that Structural Honesty's ideological bed-fellows, the Common Sense, the Practical and the Classifiable, are alive and kicking.

The traditional is an over-arching idea used in explanations of the contemporary malaise concerning building construction, as much as in more visible controversies over architectural aesthetics. The rhetoric of chartered surveyors, the industry's self-appointed trouble-shooters, squarely blames architects because '(they) abandoned traditional building construction so that simple problems that had been solved for generations reappeared with the advent of modern construction. This led not only to structural failures but aesthetic failures.'[13] The traditional is set up like the common sense, the practical and the scientific, as something we are all agreed upon.

This appeal to the traditional would suggest a simple retro step would be the best solution to building failure. But the everyday practice of housing construction has adopted the double-skinned cavity wall, not the 9-inch solid brick wall of the Victorians as its preferred configuration of the 'traditional'. If you look at it through half-shut eyes, the outside of cavity wall may look traditional, but the interior of the wall has, since the mid-1970s, accumulated more and more factory-made, additional specialist, classifiable elements which present themselves as scientific. The cavity wall was originally conceived as a straightforward answer to rain penetration; the outside leaf got wet, and the inner one stayed dry. But the 1973 oil crisis meant that suddenly the wall urgently needed to keep out cold as well as water. The response was to cram the interior with insulation. From then innovation in the constructional component industry blossomed on the back, ironically, of the idea of the 'traditional': the interior of the cavity wall now carries enough paraphernalia to furnish a post-punk boutique. Absurdly, in order to sustain a facade plain and boring enough to warrant the yearned-for label of 'traditional', the unseen interior is burdened with all the trappings of technological progress.

Rabid hydrophobia has now supplanted the apparently gung-ho attitude to water penetration of previous decades; the steel ties which hold the two skins of the wall together are contorted with drips; there are plastic 'weepholes', waterproof linings; high specification cavity trays, cavity wall 'bats', shiny plastic discs. All is protected from the slightest contaminating drop. In a different form, the 1960s' version of science exemplified in the *Architects' Journal* technical information sheets, persists. Components are examined exhaustively, but forever in isolation – in housing construction, the classification of wall ties replaces the classification of concrete panels.

Akin to the back-to-nature fashion in make-up, introduced in the 1970s, this is a reaction to the honestly technological look of the 1960s – Barbarella-style false eyelashes and bleached-out lips (see the discussion in Chapter 4). Just as in traditional building construction, the 'traditional', 'natural' no-make-up look spawns an ever-expanding range of specialist products to help sustain it behind the scenes (Fig. 2.11) – all of which appeal to a scientific sensibility while emphasising an uncontrived appearance.

## Fictional allegories and purity and tolerance

The priests of the technical induce a passive glaze in the communicants of their unchallenged 'knowledge'. As it were bombarded with facts and specialisms, we are content to accept at face value the absolute truth of the terms of technical 'knowledge'. The expression 'blinded with science' is peculiarly apposite to building construction: one feels timorous trying to see through the light. The aim here is to get at the reality that exists independently of the languages by which it is made

**2.11** Advertisement for natural make-up (1970s).

available, so that its real nature remains ineffable and hidden,[14] i.e. the reality that lurks behind tech-speak. One method that attempts this is the creation of allegorical fictions in tandem with the manipulation of materials and space. It is the subject of two architectural installations described below. Both have explored some of the issues raised by this chapter by beginning to conceive of an architecture that questions the pervasive separation, delineation and classification of constructional elements.

The Economist Building, by Alison and Peter Smithson[15] is a Brutalist icon in Central London, and home to Britain's Architecture Foundation. *Purity and Tolerance* was an allegorical installation by Muf Architects and the author, involving installation, video and text. The text made an explicit analogy between leakage in sanitary towels and leakage in system-built panelled buildings. The aim was to blow apart the constructional mystification shrouding the architectural profession and the building profession, always, implicitly, male. In an extremely posh part of London's West End, where the vast majority of passers-by are male, the following text was inscribed, and repeated, in immaculate calligraphy on the windows (Fig. 2.12) addressing the street outside:

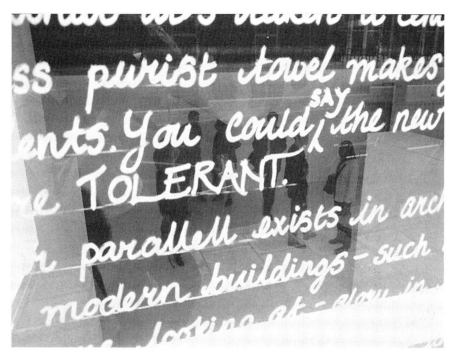

**2.12** *Purity and Tolerance* (1995): Architectural installation by Muf Architects and Katherine Shonfield, at the Economist Building, London: Text written on windows.

Until very recently most towels had straight edges.

There was something a bit token about them; in addition to being rectangular and having no overlap, they were made of one material. If that failed and you leaked any blood at all it inevitably flowed over the edge of the straight cut, and on into the outside world. Of late, wings and layers of different materials have been introduced. They distort the purity of the towel's edge, and they overlap.

It's odd that it's taken a century to accept that a less purist towel makes for a lot less accidents. You could say the new towels are a lot more TOLERANT.

A peculiar parallel exists in architecture. Panelled modern buildings – such as the one you're looking at – glory in their straight edges, and purity – only one material at a time as per the old style towel. Until quite recently some buildings weren't too bothered about how the panels joined up. If there was a lot of water around, they just leaked. Like the Emperor's New Sanitary Towels ordinary people seemed too cowed by the experts to mention this for a while.

Street lights projected the text deep into the space of the building, distorting the shadow of its words over the installation.

In the whited-out interior of the Foundation, a huge, white, shiny and seamless ceiling material was installed. It was stretched over the space and filled with water, as if the building above had leaked into it so that it bulged (Fig. 2.13).

**2.13** *Purity and Tolerance* (1995): Stretchy, shiny, white ceiling filled with water.

*Dirt is Matter Out of Place* was a temporary transformation of an interior, by the author and Frank O'Sullivan in a disused Victorian lavatory outside the great Baroque church of Nicholas Hawksmoor, Christchurch, in Spitalfields, London. The installation sought to undermine the way the architecture delineated and defined the literal production of dirt.

The accompanying text was published as a separate volume. It brought together four parallel sites of the war against dirt as matter out of place: text, architectural plans, urban scale maps, and advertisements for cleaning products (Fig. 2.14). A fictional history of the lavatory was concocted, describing its transformation through a series of 'eras'. Each era had an architectural scale orthographic plan, showing alterations to the architecture of the lavatory in response to circumstances of the battle. The equivalent battle of slum clearance and imposition of new urban borders was mapped on a wider scale in the immediate neighbourhood. The catchwords of cleaning products packages, domestic and cosmetic, were projected as transparencies over the architectural drawings. The following excerpt describes the moment of the installation:

### 6  The era of de-regulation through feathering

Dirt was surreptitiously re-introduced into the site in the form of white feathers. Vitreous sealed interior and apparatus were both spread with a homogenous cover of down, masking the crisp edge of the regularising geometry and so disordering its individual character and function. At detail level the feathers confounded the ability of the dirt-denying brick to repel its corrupting germ enemy (Fig. 2.15).

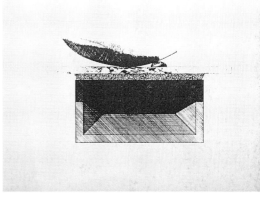

**2.14** *Dirt is Matter Out of Place* (1991): Fairy Snow washing powder transparency.

**2.15** *Dirt is Matter Out of Place* (1991): Drawing of feather detail by Frank O'Sullivan.

Inside the lavatory the application of a homogenous layer of white goose feathers irretrievably blurred the junctions between constructional categories, in an attempt to make a magical sensation of the space as one whole, as in a Baroque church, re-emerge (Figs 2.16 and 2.17).

The two installational allegories try to reveal new worlds of ingenuity for everyday construction, denied by the residue of our obsession with classes, purity and components. In the topsy-turvy world of 'traditional' house building as well, the craft and delicacy of the modern building site are all there: but with no one to see. We fiddle endlessly with the complex configurations of the cavity wall interior, merely to achieve a bland and implacable facade. Dragged into the outside air, they could be an alternative future for building construction: of invention, fun and decoration.

**2.16** *Dirt is Matter Out of Place* (1991): Installation at Christchurch, Spitalfields, London, Frank O'Sullivan and Katherine Shonfield: detail view.

**2.17** *Dirt is Matter Out of Place* (1991): Installation at Christchurch, Spitalfields, London, Frank O'Sullivan and Katherine Shonfield: general view.

## Notes

1    Greater London Council, *GLC Good Practice Details*, (London: Architectural Press, 1979).

2    Lionel Esher, *A Broken Wave: The Rebuilding of England 1940–1980*, (London: Allen Lane, 1980) p. 127.

3    Brian Finnimore, *Houses from the Factory: System Building and the Welfare State*, (London: Rivers Oram Press, 1989), p. 73.

4    See discussion in Chapter 1.

5    Cecil C. Handisyde, *Everyday Details*, (London: Architectural Press, 1976).

6    Ibid., pp. 30–2.

7    J. Carter, Architectural Adviser to the RIBA Journal, *RIBAJ* LXXIV (1967), p. 477, quoted in Brian Finnimore, op. cit., p. 103.

8    'Joints and Jointing', *Architects' Journal*, 23 April 1969, paragraph 1.02.

9    *A Day in the Life*, © Lennon and McCartney, *Sergeant Pepper's Lonely Hearts Club Band*, Parlophone Records, 1968.

10    *Architects' Journal*, 15 November 1967.

11    *Concise Oxford Dictionary*, 1963.

12    *Architects' Journal*, 26 February 1969, pp. 565–82.

13    Building Defects Supplement, *Chartered Surveyor* magazine, April 1981, p. 4.

14    A central theme of Christine Buci-Glucksmann, *Baroque Reason: The Aesthetics of Modernity*, (London: Sage, 1994); see also this book's Endpiece.

15    Economist Building, London (1964).

**Part two:** The Interior

Chapter 3
## These walls have feelings:
the interiors of *Repulsion* and *Rosemary's Baby*

> When something is firmly classed as anomalous the outline of the set in which it is not
> a member is clarified . . . the viscous is a state half way between solid and liquid. It is
> like a cross section in a process of change. It is unstable but it does not flow. It is soft,
> yielding and compressible. There is no gliding on its surface. Its stickiness is a trap, it
> clings like a leech; it attacks the boundary between myself and it. I remain a solid, but
> to touch stickiness is to risk diluting myself into viscosity.
>
> Jean-Paul Sartre's essay on stickiness, quoted by Mary Douglas in
> *Purity and Danger*.[1]

In this chapter I want to look at the smearing of the most fundamental of architectural
boundaries, between inside and outside, in two of Roman Polanski's most effective
and memorable horror films, *Repulsion* (1965), and *Rosemary's Baby* (1968).

Perhaps it is no surprise that Polanski's work should explore borders, edges
and their incursion. Until the age of four he grew up in the Cracow Jewish ghetto,
in Poland. When the Nazis came, his father lifted up the fence that was the boundary
of the edge of the ghetto, and told Roman to run. He was picked up by a pair of
elderly Catholic peasants who brought him up as their own. The young Polanski must
have looked remarkably similar to the beautiful blonde victims of *Rosemary's Baby*
and *Repulsion*. The child himself woefully failed to live up to Polish fixed definitions
of the racial characteristics of Jews, borne of their fear of smearing the boundaries of
their own perverse categories of racial purity.

Both *Repulsion* and *Rosemary's Baby* implicate the primal fear of smearing,
explored through an analogy between the interior space of their heroine's bodies,
and the interiors of the apartments where they live. In both, the transgression of the
architectural edge – the wall, the floor, the way – holds the threat of the violation of
the edge of their bodies. The films deal with fear of penetration writ large: written
on the architecture of the interior and the architecture of the cities in which the films'
action takes place: London and New York.

*Repulsion* is filmed in black and white and in London. It is Polanski's first
English language film. Unstable, but beautiful Carol, played by Catherine Deneuve,
works in a beauty salon in South Kensington. Her work itself involves smearing. She
is shown plastering over her ageing customers' cracks with thick impasto face packs.

She is a fragile, introverted virgin: her beauty attracts a slightly awed response from her boyfriend. Her sister's departure for a week in Rome with an insensitive, would-be playboy, gives the opportunity for Carol's fears of penetration to be played out, both in the city outside and in the body of her flat. In the course of the film, the surfaces of the flat start to crack, and can no longer hold back the outside. At its climax, the walls begin literally to smear the edge between Deneuve and themselves.

*Rosemary's Baby* takes place three years later, in 1968. It is filmed in colour in New York. This time, the heroine, Rosemary, played by Mia Farrow, is manifestly sane. Newly wed to a clean-cut advertising executive type, they move into their dream apartment in Manhattan's Dakota building, later home to John Lennon. The first indication that all is not what it might be in Rosemary's interior is that she can't tell where the edges of her apartment actually begin or end. These signs of architectural unease coincide with strangely intrusive neighbours, and her own reassessment of the interior borders of her body following the conception of her first child. The compromised edge of her apartment manifests itself both spatially and immaterially, in ways that are not directly visible. She becomes conscious of being spied on from the outside, she is continually assaulted by external noise penetration. The film ends with the confirmation that both architectural and bodily interiors have been violated by a group of Satanists: Rosemary's baby turns out to be not hers at all, but the Devil's.

In Chapters 1 and 2, I looked at how the archetypal architectures of the 1960s, system building and Brutalism, both carry the fantasy that an interior can become merely the other side of the wall. The implication is that the interior as a distinct, separate entity has disappeared. Against that background, *Repulsion* and *Rosemary's Baby* are the story of the vengeance of the interior. In both, the difference between inside and outside refuses to disappear, and the interior aggressively reasserts itself. Chapter 2, *Why does your flat leak?* considered this ideological dismissal of the interior as a place of discrete requirements and needs, to be a root cause of constructional problems. The depicted power of the interior in these two films can be read as a prescient cautionary tale of catastrophic building-failure-to-come.

As Sharon Marcus makes clear in her essay on *Rosemary's Baby* in *differences*,[2] the historical background to the film is an increasing anxiety about issues of security and permeability in society as a whole. She focuses in particular on the nascent awareness, contemporary with both the book and film of *Rosemary's Baby*, that the foetus is subject to outside influences, rather than hermetically encapsulated by the body of the mother, as had been assumed during the 1950s. These insights of Marcus, coupled with contemporary architectural assaults on the notion of the discrete interior, set out the background tensions within which both the architectural content of these films and developments within the technical market of building products can be understood.

In *Repulsion*, Carol's fears are concentrated on the questionable integrity of the walls of her flat. These walls – unsponsored by either the Royal Institute of Chartered Surveyors, or Architects – are nevertheless remarkable in that they explicitly demonstrate three types of constructional failure, attendant on contemporary changes in building practice in post-war London. Damp penetration, cracking of internal surfaces, and failure of mastic sealants all come under the microscopic eye of Carol's technical inspection.

In the sequence shown in Figs 3.1 and 3.2 Catherine Deneuve intently examines a damp patch (Fig. 3.1). Damp provokes an extreme form of fungal growth (Fig. 3.2). It releases what is latent and alien inside as if it were a Pandora's wall. The universal adoption of cavity wall construction in Britain post-war led to the perception of the space within the wall as a literal 'gap in the market'. Pumped formaldehyde insulation was marketed by door-to-door salesmen to fill that gap (Fig. 3.3), in the manner of double glazing, with the similar tag that it would reduce heating bills.

From the mid-1960s it became increasingly likely that your wall might contain an alien viscous substance, unseen within its apparent traditionally built solidity. Like the sprouting wall in *Repulsion*, the formaldehyde insulation emerged from the solidity of the wall in the form of toxic fumes to attack the occupants of the spaces beyond.

**3.1** *Repulsion* (1965): Catherine Deneuve examines a damp patch .

**3.2** *Repulsion* (1965): The wall has sprouted.

**3.3** Man demonstrating the pumping of formaldehyde insulation into a cavity wall.

Invading services prove too much for the integrity of the wall's internal plaster skin: it is ruptured and a massive crack instantly appears (Fig. 3.4).

**3.4**  *Repulsion* (1965): Catherine Deneuve turns the light on, and the wall cracks.

Carol flings herself against the wall as to a haven of security in the face of the threats within her apartment. She clings to it; and it begins to cling to her. She finds it melting beneath her fingertips. The wall itself acts like a monstrous mastic joint: it returns to a state of viscosity (Fig. 3.5). The architecture can no longer be relied upon to maintain 'the boundary between myself and it': in Mary Douglas' words: 'Its stickiness is a trap', and in touching it, Carol risks 'diluting herself into viscosity'. Or, in the words of an examination of mastic joint failure in 1968 the 'presence of moisture behind brick wall caused "reversion" of sealant (becomes gooey again)'.[3]

**3.5** *Repulsion* (1965): Catherine Deneuve clings to a melting wall.

During a dream scene Carol seals off her bedroom by dragging a wardrobe to block the doorway. Penetration of the blockade is signalled first by a light, and then by a man who breaks his way in. At the threshold of any breach to the membrane of her physical security, there is a man, or the threat of one. *Repulsion* is the opposite of its parallel fiction: the world of building product literature. In the product literature world, an uncompromisingly male figure accompanies and confirms the very security which, in Carol's nightmare of building failure, he undermines. The incipient language of security particularly characterises the marketing of sealants. It is as if the industry instinctively recognises the risks of the pared-down, inflexible forms of construction which have become the post-war norm: the sealant is portrayed with a masculine sense of responsibility, sole guardian of the integrity of the interior.

Thus, in this US advert (Fig. 3.6), when you buy *Lasto-Meric* you buy both the sealant and the reassuring male figure that goes with it, 'the Tremco Representative': as if he were literally a safety salesman: the pun on 'seal' is made the most of.

The form and language associated with the mastic gun, the appliance used for the application of mastic which was in general use by the late 1950s, embody the increasingly inflexible, component-based building industry's unease with this viscous product. The glossary of sealant and glazing terms for the use of mastic

Lasto-Meric,
the Thiokol Seal of Security and the
Tremco Representative.

**3.6** Advertisement for *Lasto-Meric* (1968): The Thiokol Seal of Security and the Tremco Representative.

published in *Architectural Record* (1968),[4] tells us that mastic may be made up to 'gun consistency', a 'compound made up to a degree of softness suitable for application through the nozzle of a caulking gun', and 'knife consistency', a 'compound formulated in a degree of firmness suitable for application with a glazing knife'. The finishes seek to deny the viscosity, the smearing qualities of the product, and present its finished form, through the language of violent defence (guns and knives), as something uncompromisingly protective.

By contrast, the woman washing graffiti from the Suwide-Tedlar plastic wall covering wears a nightie-like covering, no gloves, and is lit as if by Polanski himself, obliterating her individuality (Fig. 3.7). She is as distracted by the surface of the wall as Carol in *Repulsion*. The conditions to which the compound is subject when left to its own devices tell an equivalent story of feminine weakness. It acts like Catherine Deneuve left defenceless within her flat. The sealant glossary combines the technical terms of the beauty salon, the place where Deneuve works as assistant in holding back failures of the body's own external skin, with the language of feminine sensibility.

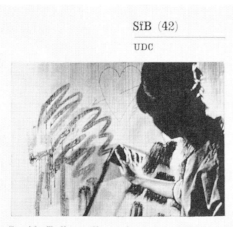

Suwide-Tedlar wall covering being washed

**3.7** *Architects' Journal*, 'Products File' (1966): Woman washing grafitti from Suwide-Tedlar plastic wall covering.

'Wrinkling – The formulation of wrinkles on the skin of a compound during the formation of its surface skin by oxidisation'; 'Weeping – Failure to support its own weight in a joint, but less pronounced than sagging'; 'Shrinking – Deficiency of a compound, when it occurs excessively in which the applied bead loses volume and contracts', and, of course, 'Bleeding – The absorption of oil or vehicle in compound into an adjacent porous surface'. The pathetic incapacity of mastic to function without controlling male containment is paralleled by the depiction of women within contemporary building product literature, which echo uncannily the hesitant fragile form of Deneuve's depiction of Carol.

This duality of viscous freedom and its rigorous containment emerges during the course of the 1960s as a self-conscious preoccupation within architectural thought. The influential work of Archigram, a group of avant-garde designers working in London, reassesses the inside and outside. It expresses the tensions between contemporary moves away from containment, rules and convention, expressed in the growing acceptance of, and fascination with, both sexual promiscuity and mind-expanding drugs, and the continued preoccupation of the profession with systematisation revealed in the continued promotion of the Modular (as opposed to the Permissive) Society by the building industry.[5] The Modular Society expressed the increasing concern, as evinced in the contemporary architectural press, with the standardisation of building components. Such fixed categorisation was seen as key to the modernisation and the future of the industry. It involved decisions of exclusion, and delineation – acts of robust assertion of the edge. The external architectural form of a number of early Archigram proposals was on a par with these concerns. The interior was depicted as a different and separate world, undulating, amorphous and directly associated with the female. Warren Chalk's 'Capsule Homes' project of 1964 shows a red soft interior, whose main domestic function is sensuous escape (Fig. 3.8).

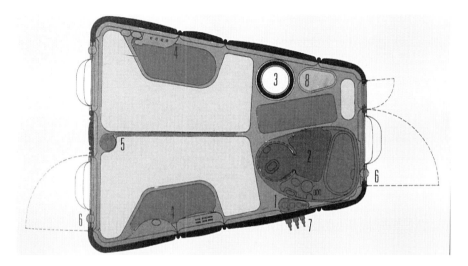

**3.8**  *Archigram* (1964): Capsule Homes project by Warren Chalk.

The reassertion of the interior takes a form similar to a static version of a *Repulsion*-like viscous wall in two projects, one in London, the other in the USA. In both, the inhabitant is explicitly invited to enter a different sphere to the matter-of-fact outside – the worlds of cinematic fantasy and of religious inspiration. The Curzon Cinema (Fig. 3.9), built in a strictly rectilinear envelope in 1965, features an aggressively three-dimensional wall which faces the cinema-goer at the point where they descend the stairs announcing a subterranean world of fantasy at odds with the outside, which, in full Cinemascope, has the intent of encompassing the sensual experience of the viewer.

A remarkable wall within a US monastery works in an analogous manner. Inscribed with the single word 'Brother', the wall seeks to detach itself from its vertical plane, and reaches out to the immediate territory of the inhabitant beyond it (Fig. 3.10). The wall here is an evangelist, seeking almost literally to grab the soul of the passer-by, after the prescribed Counter-Reformatory manner.[6]

The edges of the apartment in the film *Rosemary's Baby* are equally insistent in smearing the border between institution and inhabitant: their mission, though, is to smear the edges of the unknowing Rosemary within a Satanist, rather than Christian

**3.9** Wall in the Curzon Cinema, London (1965): Sir John Burnet, Tait & Partners.

**3.10** Wall at St Vincent's Monastery, Latrobe, Pennsylvania (1968): Tasso Katselas.

community. As in *Repulsion*, the sane world is the one where your personal edges, bodily and architectural, are firmly in place. *Rosemary's Baby* extends the architectural vocabulary of the compromised edge beyond *Repulsion*'s close focus on the integrity of the wall. Three new areas of contemporary architectural interest are introduced: sound insulation, colour co-ordination and spatial ambiguity.

On moving in, Rosemary investigates a corridor, blocked at one end, in the manner of Carol's bedroom door, by a large wooden chest of drawers. Again, as in *Repulsion*, the tell-tale light from behind indicates that here is a compromised edge; the one Rosemary has to worry about is that with her neighbour's flat. She is told that the previous tenant placed the chest there to block the way. Why block the way when there is a wall behind? On moving it, she reveals only the hum-drum inhabitants of a neglected cupboard – vacuum cleaner and household linen. In the course of film, though, her Satanist neighbours burst through this weak partition between their own and Rosemary's apartment, inexorably reinstating an original, structural and psychological link.

The advertisement for *Fol-Door* (Fig. 3.11) reveals that it is a hybridised architectural component, neither a wall nor door. It is the equivalent of the dividing partition at the end of Rosemary's corridor. While the text informs the reader that they can 'change halls into classrooms' and 'banquet areas into luncheon rooms', in the imagery of the advertisement, the rooms are domestic, and their exact function is unclear. The elimination of the door leaves the lone, seated woman oddly exposed, to a voyeuristic, and indeed filmic, gaze. *Fol-Door* permits the viewer to see further into privately occupied space than the established architectural conventions of either open door or open plan. This uneasy architectural ambiguity works in contrast to the strict control of access traditionally determined by the radius of an opening door. Since the Victorian era, the accepted swing of an opening door moves into, rather than out of, the room to be entered. The view in is momentarily shielded from the incomer: the inhabitants of the room are made aware of the intrusion and have time to present themselves appropriately.[7] This convention was just starting to change towards the end of the 1960s.[8] This meant that the door now opened against the wall of the room to be entered, exposing the entire room to the immediate view of the new visitor. In open plan living as well, the levels of exposure to the eyes of others are under the control of the person already dwelling in the interior: they behave and arrange themselves accordingly. In this sense they cannot be caught *unawares*. By contrast, in the fore of the *Fol-Door* images is the figure of a man (Fig. 3.12).

He acts like the trespasser in Carol's dream, actively moving a wall in order to enter a previously discrete space, the new spatial relations allowing penetration where it has previously been unavailable – into the contemplative zone of the neighbouring image where a woman imagines she dwells on her own.

**3.11** Advertisement for Divide or Expand *Fol-Door* (1968).

**3.12** Advertisement for Divide or Expand *Fol-Door* (1968): Close-up.

The idea of the inside as the simple reverse of the outside wall-panel is reinforced in the publicity for an *interior* vinyl wall-paper, advertised as blocks of colour on the *exterior* of a modern block of flats (Fig. 3.13). Rosemary's first act on acquiring her apartment is to start wallpapering in a cheerful, contemporary pattern. She literally papers over the cracks in the flat's edges. In the course of her redecoration the viewer finds that it has the unusual effect of colour co-ordinating Rosemary herself, not only with her new interior, but with the clothes of her demonic neighbour (Fig. 3.14). In a final twist, their chosen colours are the yellow and blue of devotional depictions of the Virgin Mary.

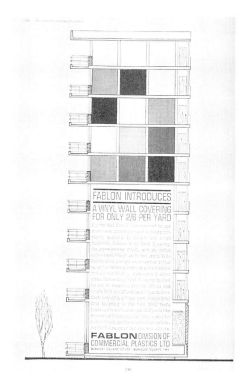

**3.13** Advertisement for Fablon vinyl wall covering (1964): Inside as Outside.

Even more insidiously than in *Repulsion*, the apparently innocent walls have swallowed up Rosemary's physical and architectural integrity. She becomes the embodiment of her own violated interior: a zone without borders. There is no longer an edge between Rosemary and her witchy neighbours, and it is only a matter of time before she fulfils her own twisted version of the Madonna role: by bearing the Devil's own son.

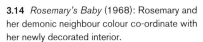

**3.14** *Rosemary's Baby* (1968): Rosemary and her demonic neighbour colour co-ordinate with her newly decorated interior.

**3.15** *Rosemary's Baby* (1968): Rosemary lying in bed listening to noise from the neighbouring apartment.

As Rosemary lies awake in her bed, the noise from her neighbours is depicted by Polanski transforming the new, deceptively innocent, flowery wall-paper of her bedroom (Fig. 3.15). When she finally sleeps, the sound manages to dematerialise the party wall: Rosemary dreams of blocking-up walls to no avail. In the architectural world of *Rosemary's Baby* the viewer learns that walls cannot be relied upon to defend borders. Thus, noise is shown in the visual language of film both penetrating and distorting. While Rosemary appears remarkably unaffected by this disturbance, in the *Architectural Record* of that year, there are no fewer than three major features dealing with the contemporary preoccupation with sound penetration.

In the professional press a diagram of flanking paths – the lines sound will take through barriers of least resistance – shows the insubstantiality of walls, floors and ceilings in the face of the power of sound's ever-penetrating arrow (Fig. 3.16). Rosemary thinks she is dreaming when she is bound hand and foot in a travesty of crucifixion, before her body is violated by the neighbouring devil-worshipper; while this contemporary diagram uses a cruciform diagram of a building to demonstrate graphically such an involuntary subjection of a physical body – built or corporeal – to the immaterial power of sound (Fig. 3.17).

*Rosemary's Baby* runs with the theme of the violation of the interior and develops it with a palette of architectural sophistication, beyond the questionable physical integrity of the wall, which preoccupies *Repulsion*. But attitudes towards the external space of the city differ markedly between the films. For Rosemary, Manhattan is her respite and relief from the fears of the interior; for Carol, the heroine of *Repulsion*, the attack on her edges continues seamlessly whether inside or outside. The difference in their attitudes to the city-at-large signifies their sanity or otherwise.

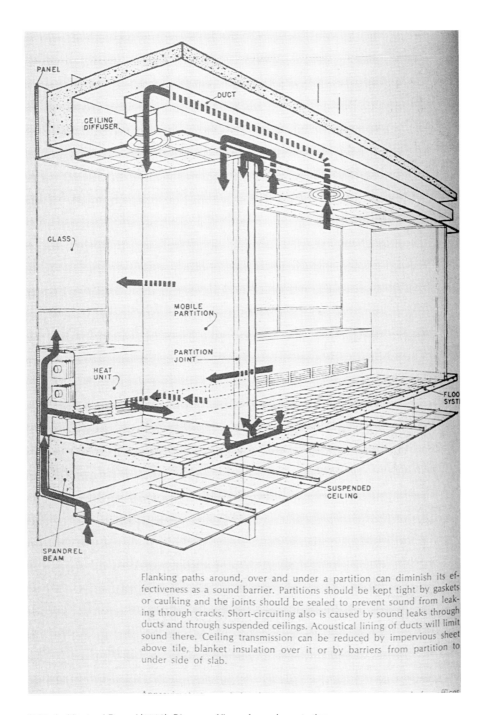

Flanking paths around, over and under a partition can diminish its effectiveness as a sound barrier. Partitions should be kept tight by gaskets or caulking and the joints should be sealed to prevent sound from leaking through cracks. Short-circuiting also is caused by sound leaks through ducts and through suspended ceilings. Acoustical lining of ducts will limit sound there. Ceiling transmission can be reduced by impervious sheet above tile, blanket insulation over it or by barriers from partition to under side of slab.

**3.16** *Architectural Record* (1968): Diagram of lines of sound penetration.

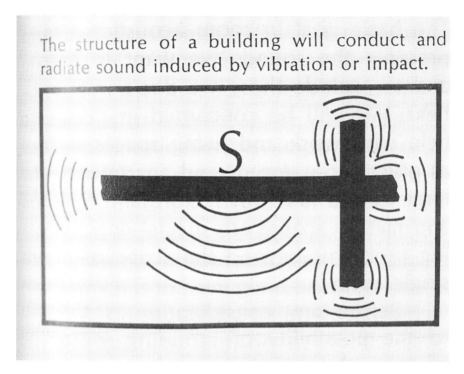

The structure of a building will conduct and radiate sound induced by vibration or impact.

**3.17** *Architectural Record* (1968): Diagram of sound conduction and radiation by a building.

It is Rosemary's lack of paranoia which means she refuses to believe the full horror of the real threats which lurk in her apartment block; their absence in the streets confirms (briefly) her own sanity. Carol is recognisably insane. She writes her fears on all the architecture that surrounds her, outside and in.

Marcus notes that the contemporary view of both the book and the film of *Rosemary's Baby* was that they ironically reversed the New Yorkers' habitual perception of their city as a terrifying unknown world, from which the home was a safe haven. More importantly than that, it is actually Rosemary's perception of the city's safety that allows the viewer to be sure she is *not* crazy. From the moment when Rosemary draws back the curtain of her unwholesomely yellow-and-blue world to gaze at the grey skyline, the whole spatial drama of the film rests on the viewer willing Rosemary to get out of the Dakota building, and into the benign city beyond. Once Rosemary is in the streets she loses her colour co-ordination. Her clothes show up as distinct edges against the equally distinct profiles of familiar building. Pale and ill, she walks alone through the streets smiling at the landmark Radio City, so different from the insidious world of her own Radio Apartment, where sound is transmitted irrespective of the listener's wishes.

Just when the viewer senses a possibility of freedom, based on escape into the city's anonymous territory, Rosemary meets her neighbour, Mrs Castavet, by chance. She is dragged back to the Dakota building. In contrast to the healthy, safe anonymity of central Manhattan, Mrs Castavet signifies an unnaturally un-urban neighbourliness. This is what Jane Jacobs calls 'togetherness' – a characteristic not of the inner-city, but of the anti-urban, the suburb where typically borders such as thresholds of apartments are not respected and there is an absence of distinction between unwarranted intimacy and good citizenship. Like Polanski, Jacobs places togetherness firmly on the dysfunctional side of evil but urban *anonymity* on the side of good.[9]

For Carol, London simply extends and varies the assault on her edges that happens inside her flat. She takes to the streets of London when it is at its most exhibitionist. In 1965 it has the eyes of the western world on it: the following year it is dubbed 'The Swinging City' by *Time* magazine.[10] Accepted street behaviour for men and women is captured in these contemporary photographs of the most famous and iconic of 1960s' London streets: Carnaby Street (Figs 3.18 and 3.19).

**3.18** Boys sitting on Vespas watching girls in Carnaby Street, London.

**3.19** (1967) Mini-skirted girls with prams parading for the men in Carnaby Street, London.

Andy Williams' song *Music to Watch Girls By* sums up the visual interplay in the streets very well: 'the boys watch the girls, and the girls watch the boys watch the girls go by'.[11] The men are sitting but their eyes move: the women move, but their gaze is constrained into a self-conscious disregard of the men's looks.

While Rosemary can drift about, looking all around her, for Carol to traverse the streets of London is an ordeal where she unavoidably faces the visual intrusion of another's eye. She mainly looks down to a cracking pavement, an urban horizontal

**3.20** *Repulsion* (1965): Deneuve crossing the road towards the workman's hut.

**3.21** *Repulsion* (1965): Torso of man outside workman's hut.

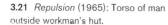

**3.22** *Repulsion* (1965): Close-up of workman's face.

equivalent to the breaches of her apartment's walls, it threatens to reveal a grotesque underground world beyond. And, like the threatened edges of her flat, the perforation of these edges of city civilisation is heralded by a male. She passes the same territory over and over: the traffic island opposite South Kensington tube station. She has to run the traditional gauntlet of the guardians of the road surface, i.e. the men who are digging it up. In this sequence, Polanski puts us as nearly as he can inside the body of Deneuve experiencing that penetrative look of a man who is so at ease in the streets he can afford to be completely static.

We watch her back and her inclined head as she crosses the road with the workman's hut in the centre of the frame: his torso, and then his face and then a close-up come into view seen through Carol's eyes (Figs 3.20, 3.21 and 3.22). Just as she is passing he mutters: 'Fancy a bit of the other, Darling?', and the relaxed face of another sitting workman staring calmly at Carol hoves into view. The final shot shows the workman leering directly at the camera. His pose is directly echoed by Alfie's in the film of the same name, released in the same year.[12] Both reveal a moment of confident appropriation of the city as a whole and its female inhabitants as legitimate territory for the male sexual adventurer. This moment is particularly remarkable: the flaneur of earlier times so commands the streets that he can sit or lounge, just as if they were his own living room. The distinction between interior and exterior has indeed begun to disappear.

## Notes

1   Mary Douglas, *Purity and Danger: An Analysis of the Concepts of Pollution and Taboo*, (London: Routledge & Kegan Paul, 1966), p. 38.

2   Sharon Marcus, 'Placing *Rosemary's Baby*', in *differences: A Journal of Feminist Cultural Studies*, (Providence, USA: Indiana University Press), vol. 5, no. 3, pp. 121–53.

3   *Architectural Record*, May 1968, p. 207.

4   *Architectural Record*, May 1968, p. 210.

5   The Modular Society, founded in 1953. See Brian Finnimore, *Houses from the Factory: System Building and the Welfare State*, (London: Rivers Oram Press, 1989), p. 149.

6   See discussion under the subtitle 'Rationality and Irrationality' in this book's Endpiece.

7   'The greatest care is also taken to see that those seated in the room are disturbed as little as possible by the opening of the door. The most important point is that people should not be disturbed and this is reflected mainly in the direction in which the door opens . . . The idea behind this is that the person entering shall not be able to take in the whole room at a glance as he opens the first crack of the door but must walk round it to enter the room, by which time the person seated in the room will have been able to prepare

himself suitably for his entry . . . The striking feature about the opening of the doors . . . is that the person entering seems at first to be walking into a wall and sees nothing inside the room until he opens the door wide. In fact it is not at all unpleasant to enter a room in this way. It is only like passing through a kind of porch or small vestibule.' Hermann Muthesius, *The English House*, edited by Dennis Sharp, (London: Crosby Lockwood Staples, 1979), p. 79.

8    See, for example, the standard texts of technical data such as *Ernst Neufert Architects' Data*, Editor Rudolf Herz, (UK: Granada Publishing, 1973), p. 85.

9    Jane Jacobs, *The Death and Life of Great American Cities: The Failure of Town Planning*, (London, Penguin, 1965), p. 73.

10   'London – the Swinging City', by Piri Halsz, *Time* magazine, 15 April 1966.

11   *Music To Watch Girls By*: Velona/Ramin, Keith Prowse Music Publishing Co.

12   See Chapter 5.

Chapter 4
# Wives and lovers:
the 1960s' office interior: *Alfie*, *The Apartment* and *Darling*


The domination of capital over labour is basic to the capitalist mode of production – without it, after all, surplus value could not be extracted and accumulation would disappear. All kinds of consequences flow from this, and the relation between labour and the built environment can be understood only in terms of it. Perhaps the single most important fact is that industrial capitalism, through the reorganisation of the work process and the advent of the factory system, *forced a separation between place of work and place of reproduction and consumption.*[1] (emphasis added)

**4.1** Advertisement for the *Daily Mirror* (1964): The split between home and work.

Walter Benjamin's writings on Paris in the 19th century are the catalyst both for this chapter and much of the rest of the book.[2] His work juxtaposes economic reality, intuition, and cultural fiction; it inspires extrapolation into unknown territories nearer the present day; it provokes a multidimensional view of the impact of modernity in the city.

Notwithstanding this model of multidimensionality, my own understanding of this approach is that it is still at bottom materialist. Economics, material circumstances, such as the level and kind of production within an industry, and the physical world itself, *set the limits* within which a series of cultural possibilities may operate. In this chapter, the prerequisites for the changing nature of London's domestic and office interior are the two world war economies. The effective suspension of the market during war-time leads to the most efficient use of resources possible, and as a consequence women were actively engaged in labour outside the home. The office boom of the 1950s and 1960s meant that women again left the home, by *force majeur* – a flooded job market.

When Benjamin evokes Paris's transformation in the second half of the 19th century by Baron Haussmann, he talks of the *material* change to the urban fabric – the building of wide, straight boulevards and internal arcades, plunging through the labyrinth of the old medieval city. Specifically, he says that:

> Before Haussmann, wide pavements were rare, and the narrow ones afforded little protection from vehicles. Strolling could hardly have assumed the importance it did without the arcades.[3]

Benjamin's method sets the material context which circumscribes the possibilities of the new city: the transformation of street patterns, a material change which emanated ultimately from economic necessity. Within that context, he chooses to focus on a kind of ideal type of new urban inhabitant, the stroller whom the new boulevards allow to drift without inhibition or conscious aim through the body of the city. In this chapter, the characters of Alfie and Darling are extracted from the films of the same name. They are read as latter-day archetypal strollers through the territory of another revised city: post-war London. Against these strollers' personification of urban free movement, you can read the new physical permeability, both of the new city and its inhabitants. Benjamin himself suggests the detective as the fictional version of the stroller or flaneur: Baudelaire's most famous poem, *The Passer By*, intimates that the stroller who feelingly fantasises about a stranger in the street, is more lover than detective. He is someone who strolls at random in search of the chance, anonymous encounter. 'Promiscuous', a word that achieved a currency in the 1960s as a blunter version of ubiquitous 'permissive', decisively describes the stroller's movement through the city. *Promiscuous*: 'Consisting of members or elements of different kinds massed together without order; of mixed and disorderly composition or character'.[4] *Alfie* and *Darling*'s antecedent is Don Giovanni, albeit with a touch of Sherlock Holmes: a truly modern internationalist who puts it about ad lib among the nations, just as Alfie does in the London Boroughs.

### The revised interior and the division between home and work

> For the private citizen, for the first time the living-space became distinguished from the place of work. The former constituted itself as the interior. The office was its complement. The private citizen who in the office took reality into account, required of the interior that it should support him in his illusions . . . From this sprang the phantasmagorias of the interior.[5]

Crudely put, without Haussmann's work, in particular the construction of the boulevards, the expansion of Paris to the point where a sizeable physical and temporal gap appears between *work* and *home* would not have happened. Benjamin indicates an interplay between the modernising changes to the physical and economic city, and changes in the nature of the domestic interior. This chapter explores this interconnection between inside and outside in the context of post-war London and New York.

The division between home and work has its impact on the sexes and their territories: women at home are in charge of, and in a sense embody, the decorative interior. In contrast is the man at work and the male flaneur who can inhabit the city as his own expanse, placed between two interior worlds, the domestic and work. So, the fate of the interior in the 1950s and 1960s is intertwined with what happens to the exterior: the revised physical form of the post-war city, and in particular the means to move through the city's – and its inhabitants' – *body*.

### Woman and the interior

'The phantasmogoria', Benjamin's escapist interior that supports the office worker 'in his illusions' is rediscovered in the English home of the 1930s. This zone presided over by woman had been an established feature of bourgeois life for over three-quarters of a century. Griselda Pollock quotes Jules Simon, a French republican politician writing in 1892:

**4.2**  Women adorning various household objects with paint (1930).[6]

> What is man's vocation? It is to be a good citizen. And woman's? To be a good wife and a good mother. One is in some way called to the outside world, the other *is retained for the interior*.[7] (emphasis added)

Pollock notes that with the building of suburbs, the separation between home and work becomes concrete on an urban scale, and spatially, women's and men's distinct geographical domains are marked. The war work of 1914–1918 released the woman from the home. However, the peace and growing post-war unemployment produced the demand for women to make way for men in the office. In the 1930s tensions rise between a resurgence in demand for female clerical employment and the requirements of the home. Huge growth in London's commuter system means home becomes more separated from work, and more often sited in a suburban scape, where the home's interior is the sole distinguishing landmark of individuality in a sea of exterior similarity. Labour-saving gadgets freed the woman at home from both domestic chores and the company of domestic servants. They made the pre-war home a place ripe for seeking out new sites for perfecting the interior. The 1930s' woman has found new sites in her body for decoration (lips, hands): and hitherto satisfactory household objects are perfected with a surface application of paint, just as she had begun to do with her nails (Fig. 4.2). This decorating and decorative woman is projected onto the feminised interior via her *housework* in creating that interior. She herself becomes a furnishing, a 'meuble', for the moment, fixed in the interior, but in time movable.

## Woman, the interior and the idea of the factory

After the first world war, but before the second, the over-laden interior of the home supports the male office worker in his illusions, in the manner suggested by Benjamin. It carries the comforts that are lost at work. These terms are categorically reversed in an advertisement for Mazda lights which appeared in *Modern Homes*, a manual on interior and exterior domestic architecture aimed at the general public, three years after the end of the second world war: 'Factories and workshops have found that good work depends on good light. Surely the "workshop" in your home deserves the same consideration?' (Fig. 4.3).[8] To the woman who has been actively engaged in useful communal war work, the home sustains the illusion of the now *absent place of work*. The kitchen presents itself as a workshop, in attempt to make the home (and its attendant commodities) attractive again to the domestically emancipated woman. The advertisements in *Modern Homes* suppress the feminine aura, associated with the domestic: they list specifications of products for sale in favour of the commodity's apparent capacity *to do the job*. In the advertisement's factory/workshop, the woman looks companionably out of the picture frame, placing herself as a model to the community of women rather than a desired reflection in a mirror.

**4.3** Advertisement for *Mazda* lights (1948): 'In a sense the kitchen is the control room for the whole house.'

But as we have seen in earlier chapters, by the 1960s the boom in construction meant that not only did the interior of the home hark back to the factory; the exterior came from one. In the system-built high rise block, in logical progression from pioneering Brutalist works such as Hunstanton School, the interior is merely the flip side of the panel.[9] Far from being a place differentiated from the milieu of work five miles away or more, the interior of the new homes scarcely distinguished itself from the exterior – rarely as much as five inches away (Figs. 4.4 and 4.5).

In Chapter 2, I noted the fantasy of system building: rather than messy, noisy, dirty builders, the ideal was 'white coated, well paid workers, slotting and clipping standard components into place in rhythmic sequence on an orderly, networked and mechanised site to a faultless programme without mud, mess, sweat or swearing'.[10] In system building the factory defines both the method and the aesthetic of domestic environments: but this quotation by the RIBA Journal Architectural Adviser unwittingly reveals not the *factory* but the *automised office* as the ideal type for the future of construction. The crisp, unsullied 'white coated workers' do not mess the edges of things: and like office workers, neither sweat nor swear. In the Bison system diagram (Fig. 4.5), this new form of construction is depicted quite literally *without an interior*. Even the wall itself tries as hard as it can to be a mere line, without any thickness.[11]

## The decorative woman and the interior

The contemporary diagrams from *Homes of Today and Tomorrow* (1963), discussed in Chapter 1 (Fig. 1.18), construct the fiction of the city as a territory of fixed objects, generically similar. They, like the system buildings which house them, are matter of fact, factory-produced, un-picturesque, clear in both their edges and their purpose, without mystery. The effective elimination of the idea of the interior means that through this territory, the flow – the arrow-headed swirls of the Parker Morris diagram – can penetrate unhindered by the edge, from the largest to the smallest objects, from domestic electrical appliances to the landscapes of the remodelled modern city – with promiscuous freedom.

In Benjamin's terms, the decorative domestic interior worked as a kind of solace to the raw realities of the work place; it healed the rift between home and work making the atomised world tolerable. Now, there is no longer an interior – it is dissolved and dispersed. What happens to the impetus to mend the home/work schism with decorative fantasy? It retreats further – literally – into the interior. The woman herself has taken into herself the phantasmagoria of interiority, and of the decorative, and she now *embodies* it in, and on, her surface.

**4.4** *Architectural Review* (1956): An interior in the sky.

**4.5** (below) *Architects' Journal* (1962): Bison Wall-Frame System: diagram showing logic of the interior organisation of a block constructed using panels.

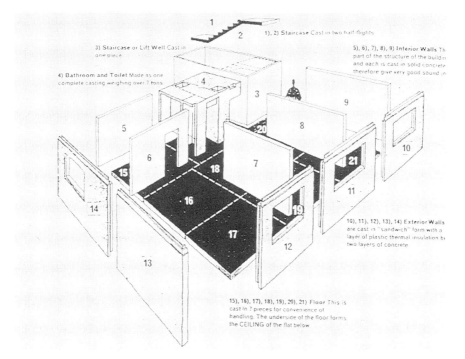

**4.6** Advertisement for Thames Board
Mills Limited 'Smooth surface cartons'
(1969): Decorative surface embodied
on the woman.

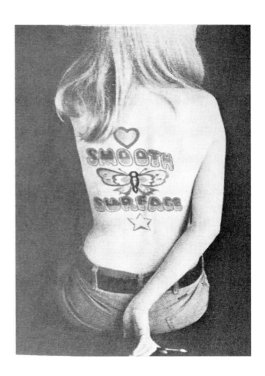

**4.7** *Vogue* (1969): Emphasising the eyes
and suppressing the mouth.

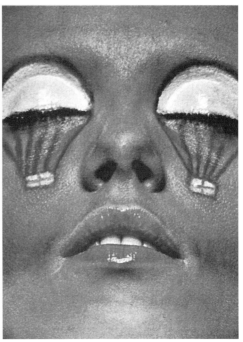

In the 1960s advertisement for Thames Board Mills (Fig. 4.6), the woman's body is used as a site for the decorative inscription of the sensuous 'phantasmagoria' officially excised from the surface of the reduced interior–exterior world.

For the woman to function effectively as a kind of movable interior decoration, her individuality must not interfere with what is communicated by her surface. In the make-up of the same period the mouth is suppressed, and blotted out in favour of the eyes, the sole site of movement (Fig. 4.7). She must shut up: in recompense is told that she can speak with her make-up instead of her mouth. In an analogous manner, the windows of the system-built tower block take on the absent decorative role of the interior. Framed in the remorseless rhythm of panelling systems, the variety wrought by the animation and different inhabitations within is thrown into relief. The entrance is suppressed in favour of windows through which movement can be viewed as abstracted, detached patterns without meaning.

**4.8** Balfron Tower (1968): Ernö Goldfinger: Emphasising the windows and suppressing the entrance.

### '*Alfie*, the interior and the city'

'Amid the deafening traffic of the town . . . tall and slender, a flash then night . . . we might have loved'.[12] Benjamin reminds us that the anonymous female passer-by of Baudelaire's poem can't exist without the anonymity of the city-wide boulevards which form the centre of the city we know today. The entire body of the city, and potentially the woman, are available to the man who drifts, untraceable, through the city from encounter to encounter.

In *Alfie* (1966),[13] the film which made Michael Caine a star, he plays a successful womaniser with the run of London. Alfie is the ultimate flaneur or drifter, whose very name conjures up a homogeneous city like a sea, on which he can float hither and thither buoyed up, without direction. But unlike the Baudelairean flaneur, he also signifies the pinnacle of a prevalent male type, familiar since the 17th century – a Don Juan: a nymphomaniac feted in literature and, up until the 1960s, severely punished – in the end – for his transgression of established lines between inside and outside. Unlike the flaneur, his quarry cannot be the female passer-by: he cannot risk the possibility that she is as mobile as himself. His licence is dependent not only on an absence of communication between the women themselves, but also on the predictability of their immobility within their assigned place, the prerequisite which allows Alfie to drift with impunity around the city sampling Woman.

In doing so, Alfie, the latter-day Don Giovanni, is aided by his very own Leporello in the form of the new building materials that transform the experience of wandering through the city.

In this sequence (Figs 4.9 to 4.11), Alfie is walking down a traditional London street past typical shop-frontages, only to be negotiated via a complex set of thresholds. Looking for an opportunity, he comes across the new plate glass window

**4.9** *Alfie* (1966): Alfie walking down a traditional London street.

**4.10** *Alfie* (1966): The new plate glass window of the new-style dry cleaners: a girl beckons him in.

**4.11** *Alfie* (1966): Alfie slips in and turns 'open' into 'closed'.

of a new-style dry cleaners. It is the thinnest possible, most transparent wall – and yet it is still a wall and provokes an intricate dance with the assistant on the other side around the theme of inside, and outside, and not quite either. He knocks on the window; she turns round, they play with touching with the glass wall in between; Alfie, arrow-like, imperceptibly slips in. By turning the open sign to closed, the transformation of public to private space is achieved with the most minimal of architectural interference.

In Alfie's world, women are types who have the abstracted status like of the mass produced commodities of the Parker Morris diagram in Chapter 1 (Fig. 1.18). He floats from interior to interior. Like a fantasy of the flowing arrow in the diagram, he can pop in and out at will. He turns the new high rise into one more object, presented for penetration, miraculously dissolving walls, obliterating distinctions of inside and outside, woman and apartment alike. In the city of post-war London, as in the Parker Morris diagram, scale is no object to Alfie the nimble arrow. Like the man digging up the street in *Repulsion*,[14] he addresses his admiring spectator audience face on, smirking: irrespective of whether he is inside or outside the building (Figs. 4.12 to 4.15).

His cocky gaze ensures the same status to the object – building and woman both – without or within. In visiting his varied sites throughout the city: Shelley

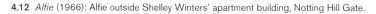

**4.12** *Alfie* (1966): Alfie outside Shelley Winters' apartment building, Notting Hill Gate.

4.13 *Alfie* (1966): Alfie outside Shelley Winters' apartment.

4.14 *Alfie* (1966): Alfie in a traditional street of terraced houses.

**4.15** *Alfie* (1966): Alfie inside a tower block.

**4.16** *Alfie* (1966): Alfie on the south side of the Thames Embankment.

Winters, the upmarket 'mature crumpet';[15] Jane Asher, the adolescent victim; Vivien Merchant, the downtrodden housewife; he moves: the woman doesn't. She is immobilised, identified with and of the interior. By contrast, Alfie possesses the city – London – and with the authority of an MP called upon to comment on the Nine O'Clock News on the specialist subject *London Birds*, he is repeatedly portrayed along the Thames Embankment, against the background of its most recognisable monuments (Fig. 4.16).

Alfie's gentle undoing is significantly heralded by his meeting with his own equivalent of *La Passante*. At the end of the film, a former girlfriend, played by Millicent Martin, who is apparently herself strolling along by the river, thwarts Alfie's casual pass. The female passer-by's role in *Alfie*'s denouement is to detach herself from the interior. She introduces a new possibility of tit-for-tat in the modern territory of 1960s' London. But, as I noted in the previous chapter, the Capsule Homes project of the contemporary avant-garde architectural group Archigram, reveals a more nostalgic view of feminity and the domestic interior.

In Fig. 4.17 the *Passer By* – 'The Passing Presence' – is transformed into an early 1960s' floozy to demonstrate the principle of 'Situation in the Living City': 'situation may occur with a change of weather, the time of day or night. As the spectator changes the moving eye sees.'[16] The spectacle presented to 'the moving eye' here, as in many of Archigram's images of a free-flowing, flexible urban ideal, is the female. The incongruity of the anonymous, hard city and the intimacy of the sexual encounter characterises the growing reality of 1960s' London, a place where such encounters become more and more available.

### *The Apartment* (1960): The flaneur in the office landscape

London's office boom was slow to come about. The incoming post-war Labour government restricted office building via a system of licences that were difficult to acquire, and by a height restriction of maximum 80 feet.[17] Again, a concerted effort was made to get women out of the jobs they had occupied in war-time, and back into the home.[18] Many banks and insurance companies operated the semi-official 'Marriage Bar', as did the Civil Service and the London County Council: the 'Marriage Bar' meant women workers were forced to resign their jobs on marriage. The 'Marriage Bar' had been lifted during the war and then put straight back into place. A woman worker in Whitehall:

> It was wartime when I got married and I had to stay on because they were short of staff, but it was very humiliating for I was immediately made a temporary member of staff and lost my pension rights.[19]

4.17 Archigram (1963): The Passing Presence.

In spite of this, although the majority of workers pre-war were men, by the late 1940s almost half of the office workers were women, but in the low positions of typists, telephonists, filing clerks and secretaries. The new Conservative government of 1951 soon got rid of restrictions and the boom began, based on growing world trade, new Welfare State bureaucracies, and London's status as one of the least tax-restrictive financial centres in the world. Mega-projects beyond Archigram's wildest dreams were proposed by apparently sober commercial architects such as the hugely successful

Richard Seifert.[20] In Manhattan, as in London, banks and insurance companies continued to be particularly attracted to the city.

Movies like *The Seven Year Itch* (1955)[21] set the tone for the era. The theme was females available for the hopeful philanderer, left on his own in the big, anonymous city. Manhattan wasn't subject to an office boom like London: while its office population continued to grow post-war, it did so at a slower rate than other areas of New York City.[22] Manhattan was already familiar with big corporate offices and their female workforce. During the first half of this century, the offices of Metropolitan Insurance's workforce of over 3,000 were segregated by function and gender. Men and women were only allowed to work together in a few supervised areas. Official guidelines proscribed a rigid dress code for women at work and specifically 'prohibited them from taking down their hair at work',[23] which must be the precursor for the classic moment in many US films where the secretary leaves the business behind and enters intimacy with a masterful removal of one hair pin.

*The Apartment* (1960)[24] is an ironic take on the opportunities for casual sexual encounter for would-be flaneurs in the office city of New York. The scene of activity is both a literal and formal microcosm of Manhattan itself: the vast, gridded and horizon-less territory of the 19th floor of a life insurance office with 31,329 employees.[25] According to the film's hero, C.C. Baxter: 'That's more than the entire population of Nachez Mississippi'. The numbered section and the numbered desk where he works are analogous with the anonymity of Manhattan's own numbered road system.

The film's twists depend on contemporary contradictory experiences within New York. Manhattan, at the centre of the archetypal 20th-century city, has anonymity in stacks. But the split between home and work has reached such a pitch that the majority of senior executives in the office population, who would be best placed to take advantage of Manhattan's drifting opportunities, live well away from the centre in places like Nassau.[26] Unlike Alfie, the chauffeur whose activities with housewives are facilitated by the office day, they have commuted to Manhattan without their cars.[27] They can gawp at hundreds of anonymous available women within the vast terrain of the office: but they can neither consume nor consummate. This is still the 1950s, and the pretence of a caring encounter, though slipping, has to be maintained. Hotels are out of the question.[28] The five guys on whom Baxter depends for his promotion all need his apartment for their sexual activity – appearances must be kept up – even if, as one tipsy blonde being yanked up the steps of the Brownstone building remarks, 'Say, are you sure your *mother* lives here?'.

In the course of the film *The Apartment* systematically pulls apart the wished-for myth of the anonymous sexy encounter at the office. It is achieved as much by the film's architectural and urban set-up as by the plot. In order for his colleagues to take advantage of these spontaneous *La Passante*-style moments in his apartment, Baxter has to stomp around the street outside, exposing himself to the derision of the neighbourhood. And these conspicuous circumstances naturally provoke the neighbourhood's re-emergence from the soup of urban anonymity, to voice its disapproval as blonde after blonde is observed emerging from the flat. He has about as much privacy as Rosemary in Polanski's version of the Dakota.[29] The internal planning of the Brownstone means Baxter has to pass his neighbour on the same landing. Its construction means that all the goings-on in the apartment are heard and attributed to Baxter, who in consequence is requested by his doctor neighbour to leave his remarkable body to science. In gridded New York and within the vast, gridded office, there is a structure allowing for free floating circulation where communication is on the phone and unavoidable physical proximity is restricted to the lift. By contrast, both the plan of the Brownstone as architectural type, and its position with its front door directly onto the street impose a high level of identifiability and hence accountability on its inhabitants. It is only Baxter's friends who 'can use his flat like a hotel'. The film poses an inner-urban condition that thwarts the aspirations of the wannabe flaneur, and traps him, willy-nilly into following up the consequences of his actions.

## Women, the office and power: feminised interiors

The mass offices of London and Manhattan are territories of unforeseen anonymity. Paradoxically at the same time they enclose a well-kept secret: the realisation of an idealised, feminised interior, rife with surface sensuality.

In London, the traditional office milieu in the years following the end of the second world war was something like Fig. 4.18.

The 'Marriage Bar' contributed to the pervasive stereotype of the female office worker as a frumpy spinster.[30] But by the mid-1960s, the stereotype had changed to Fig. 4.19.

A huge influx into the centre of young, underpaid women was a result of London's office boom; lack of equal pay legislation meant that they were a cheap labour pool. Nevertheless, they had ready money, they were in demand and they brought attitudes unfamiliar to the respectable spinster of former years.

Mini-skirted and made-up, they embodied a portable interior phantasmagoria, a new design furnishing that was commonly referred to as 'brightening the place up'. Unlike the conquests of Alfie's fantasy territory, economic demand decreed that these women didn't stay put. Office labour was a seller's market, and it brought about the era of the 'temp'. The 'temp' was a woman who was content to make a career of

**4.18** The Sun Alliance Insurance Company, London (1955).

**4.19** Mini-skirted secretary sitting on a desk with a 'modesty board', a side panel which blocked views of exposed legs, date (1960s).

temporary work. She could pick and mix her own terms of employment within the city, and move whenever she felt like it: someone with the potential to become a female flaneur of the office. 'The temp symbolised the new-found restless freedom. Freedom to move about, not to spend too long in any one place; freedom to meet new people.'[31] The architecture of the office was disrupted to accommodate their mass, rather than individual, presence:

> We all wore very short skirts – it would have been rather odd not to have done – and some were in very bright colours. This caused embarrassment for some of the men and excitement for others. Some of them couldn't stop staring at your legs so we had modesty boards arranged on all the desks . . . It became one of the perks of a job – you not only asked for rather a good salary and an electric typewriter, but also modesty boards. And if there were no modesty boards then you might re-negotiate the salary.[32]

Fig. 4.19 shows a mini-skirted young woman sitting on a desk, secure in the confidence that she can control the exposure of her body when she determines. Adrian Forty, in *Objects of Desire*, chronicles the minute architecture of the desk as a site for

**4.20** Advertisement for *Hille* office furniture (1961): The exposed office desk.

There's a Status desk for non-stop directors,

. . . for dedicated young executives

and for pretty typists

the negotiation of power within the office. As the office is more and more subject to 'scientific rationalisation' as the century goes on, the desk flattens and becomes more and more exposed. In the case of the operative, high status comes to correlate with the number of unexposed drawers – literally and figuratively.[33] Forty illustrates this in an advertisement from 1961 for the Hille office desk range (Fig. 4.20).

The advertisement graphically shows the diminishing status of diminishing architectural cover – and its physical consequences: the two men are rather too close for comfort around the pretty typist: they are both handling her fully exposed documents. There is no place for either them or her to hide. Small wonder that the achievement of a modesty board, whose leg-hiding qualities are in this advert reserved for the 'Status desk for non-stop directors', was, in the spatial language of the office, regarded as something of a triumph.

The advertisement demonstrates how the territory of the office had become overtly eroticised. In Jack Jones's hit song from the early 1960s, *Wives & Lovers*,[34] women themselves personify the split between work and home.

> Day after day there are girls at the office
> And men will always be men
> Don't think because there's a ring on your finger
> You'll ever see him again
> For wives should always be lovers too
> Run to his arms the moment he comes home to you
> I'm warning you

Jones's authoritatively male voice assumes that the same woman cannot be in the office and be within the home. If so, how could she perform the impossible act of running to her husband's arms the moment he comes home? The wife is in the home: the lover is at work. In this fiction of office life, to heal the rift between home and work, the woman must not move from the home, but must nevertheless encompass the decorative characteristics of the lover – that is, the glamorous woman as presented within the office. The office is a place for 'women who work and dress from the skin out daily! . . . They don't need a chest filled with lingerie – they dress up every day.'[35] *Wives & Lovers* goes on to warn: 'comb your hair, fix your make up . . . don't see him off with your hair still in curlers . . . you may not see him again'.

In *A Guide for the Married Man* (1967),[36] Walter Matthau's wife is impossibly good-looking and ever-ready-for-sex. Matthau has to be taught how to be unfaithful: having received his full set of lessons, he is still unable to go through with it. Having decided on fidelity, urban and architectural circumstances which tempt potentially promiscuous drifting, however, remain. The last shots of the film satirise the reality of suburban existence for many. Walter is depicted desperately maintaining his purity by avoiding all opportunity for the chance meeting. Confronted with the crowded street he rushes into the office; confronted with the office free-for-all, he rushes to the fire escape. The only way he can avoid the problem is to seal the gaps between leaving the wife/domestic interior, and rushing back to the domestic interior/wife, and reduce the entirety of the rest of life to a panic-stricken blur.

The London office boom not only flooded the market with low grade clerical jobs for women: 'Junior executive' posts also expanded. A cheap (thus young and inexperienced) secretary became an expected perk.[37] Running counter to the general trend of the period, for ever greater office automation, and the increasing regulation of clerical work through architectural means, such as open plan offices, young people of the opposite sex were thrown together in a condition of extreme one-to-one intimacy. In *The Apartment* the pinnacle of achievement in Baxter's corporation is the key to the executive washroom: there was a premium on enclosed and excluding space in the horizonless office landscape. The seclusion of the individual office became part of a newly idealised interior, wholly different from the industrialised ambience of the typing pool where the mass of women's clerical work still went on well into the late 1970s.[38] This romanticised version of a home appears in the places where women's power is completely excluded. The interior architecture of the Executive Reception and Boardroom becomes inscribed with the signs of comfort – visibly supporting the executives 'in their illusions' while they are still at work. It is also the decorative setting for the decorative adjunct – 'the girls at the office', the Non-Wife.

**4.21** Architect Richard Seifert's office, London (1967).

The architect Richard Seifert's own office is a splendid example. Seifert was the most commercially ruthless, certainly the most successful, architect of the office blocks which transformed London's skyline during this period: he ran a huge commercial concern. *Building* magazine published the image as part of an article on Seifert.[39] It reveals a wholly different aesthetic to 'just the flip side of the wall'. The interior here is a separate entity, it is a clear insertion, which belies rather than reveals the hard constructional reality beyond it. Not only does it sport easy chairs, occasional table, suspended ceiling and curtains, but the entirety of one wall is mysteriously padded and buttoned (Fig. 4.21).[40]

**4.22** The boardroom at Space House, London: architect, Richard Seifert.

Less lavishly, a Seifert boardroom at Space House, the headquarters of the Civil Aviation Authority in Central London (Fig. 4.22), has aquired the traits of home rather than work. The emphasis, in sharp distinction to the precast concrete elements of the exterior, is all on the sensuous qualities of surface, inviting touch. It is lined with luxurious timber panelling; it incorporates built-in storage banished from the architecture of the open plan office where it is all important to allow the interior its visible integrity as 'other side of the wall'. This is a secret interior world existing in opposition to the declared aesthetic of the time. One particular element in the new interior appears to be purely symbolic of the absent home. This is the office version of the sideboard or 'credenza' (Fig. 4.23).

It appears as a remnant of the time when traditionally this dresser displayed household wealth in the form of plate, to give you credence, or as in current street slang, credibility – hence 'credenza'.[41]

Like the executive desk, where, as Forty says 'the drawers . . . would normally be empty, but they did not dare suggest doing away with them',[42] the credenza for the display of riches is bereft of all real, tangible wealth. It is as if it has flown in from an idealised kitchen: a feminine magic carpet object which, like the advert for its counterpart (Fig. 4.24), can miraculously span the rift between office and home.

**4.23**  Credenza at Space House, London: architect, Richard Seifert.

**4.24**  Gerstner, Gredinger & Kutter Catalogue of modular fittings (1964): The office-and-home sideboard.

A decade earlier, in 1954, Audrey Hepburn in *Sabrina Fair*,[43] ventures in from Long Island to visit a workaholic Humphrey Bogart in his boardroom in downtown Manhattan. The magical properties of the unused boardroom sideboard come into their own as a little bit of home. In Bogart's boardroom, this apparently redundant object turns out to be first a drinks cabinet. Then, shedding her outdoor wear, Audrey

**4.25** *Sabrina Fair* (1954): Bogart with boardroom table and sideboard.

**4.26** *Sabrina Fair* (1954): Hepburn puts her apron on.

**4.27** *Sabrina Fair* (1954): Hepburn makes dinner.

reinvents herself as a housewife donning an apron and the cabinet is magically metamorphosed into the domestic kitchen. Its contents – apparently fit for nothing but a cocktail – transform, at the hand of this mistress of the domestic – she trained in Paris – into a gourmet meal (Figs 4.25 to 4.27).

In the denouement of *Sabrina Fair*, the boardroom becomes the site where all is right with the world; and the rift between home and work is healed. Instead of the panic-stricken erasure of the world of work and the city that concludes *A Guide for the Married Man*, in *Sabrina Fair* the home comes to the office and cures it of its barren, unwholesome character.

### Room at the top: views of urban order from the feminised interiors of male power

Unlike Humphrey Bogart under the benign influence of Audrey Hepburn, the mortal Londoner experienced the office boom as the opposite of a balm: on the urban scale, it irrevocably disrupted the established order of her world.

In the city which Christopher Wren attempted to create, after the mid-17th-century fire, order was understood from street level. As revealed in his post-fire plan for London, the eye is directed from Wren church to Wren church (Fig. 4.28). In the second half of the 20th century this plan is upset, apparently rendering the city orderless and incomprehensible.

But in Richard Seifert's new city, order can be understood once again – not from the street but from the tops of his office buildings. The view from the Room at

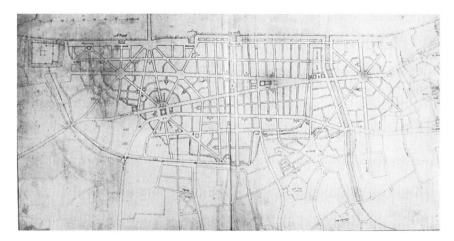

**4.28** Wren's Plan for London (1666).

**4.29** Aerial view of office building around Wren's St Paul's Cathedral in the City of London (1970).

the Top is to other rooms at the top, from Seifert boardroom to Seifert boardroom. This is especially so at night where the discreet architectural hierarchy of the office block reveals the boardroom distinguished from the repetitive forms of the floors below by its lighting. The rent within the city fabric torn by office expansion is healed, with the ointment of the view from the feminised boardroom interior. It is available only to men.

Much of this book revolves around the deep ambiguities of the 1960s manifest in apparently contradictory tendencies, pulling in different ways. *Repulsion*, *Rosemary's Baby*, *Alfie* and *The Apartment* all show that these are nowhere more evident than in the incompatible roles which women are expected to play. At the heart of the profoundly misogynistic film *Darling*, as in Emile Zola's novel *Nana*, which I will examine in the next chapter, is an amoral woman. She wreaks havoc and destruction on all around her. As in Zola's novel, the film itself holds its own deep ambiguities. While both thoroughly, and rather nastily, punish their free-living women at the end, they also revel in their similarly innocent blonde beauty and their amorous and societal conquests. In a sense the character of Darling, played by Julie Christie, epitomises the unease arising from the beginnings of a breakdown in the 1960s between a lady and a whore. The film resolves this by rejecting both.

Darling inhabits the city as if she were Baudelairian man. She is the female counterpart of Alfie: she exploits the rifts of modernisation which allow her to go from chance encounter to chance encounter. Loosely attached to journalist Dirk Bogarde for most of the film, Darling leaves her man typing, alone in the home. She

**4.30** *Darling* (1965): The new office development at Paternoster Square, London.

is always depicted as uncomfortable within the domestic interior, most memorably in a famous scene where she flings off her clothes to run shrieking through her vast, newly aquired Italian villa.

She picks up a senior executive at a party, and in full evening dress, sails regally through the flagship of the re-built post-war city, the now demolished office development opposite St Paul's Cathedral, called Paternoster Square (Fig. 4.30).

An unassuming door labelled 'Suite' leads to the interior of the boardroom. 'Suite' is an ambiguous word: it applies to office and home; the luxury it suggests encompasses both. It is most often used in hotels, places which often hang between office and home, taking up the roles of both, but which lose their associated social constraints. Darling enters a padded, soft world of yielding surfaces, generically the same as her dress, but a place from which she is normally excluded. She throws off her high heels, and starts feeling the appropriately named shag-pile carpet with her toes. Night-time emphasises the sense that she is an intruder: she goes on to transgress the symbolic sites of exclusion within the suite itself, the softened icons of the ideal romanticised boardroom interior. This, like the interior of the house in *Beat Girl* (Figs. 1.15 and 1.16), holds a secret space between inside and outside. Christie reveals the secret which lurks behind the padded wall in the Seifert reception by sliding it back to discover a closed safe, the hidden place, presumably, holding the wealth absent from the credenza (Fig 4.31).

**4.31** *Darling* (1965): Darling slides back the padded wall in the boardroom suite.

The scene ends in a cute reversal. Christie mounts the boardroom table (Fig. 4.32) to gaze down at the executive seated beneath her.

Darling transgresses work; she has transgressed home by absenting herself. The version of femininity which she brings to the boardroom does not just 'brighten the place up': it disrupts the silent and compliant feminine aspects of the soft interior. It is only momentary: and she, as we have seen, is punished for her trespassing activities. At the high point of their scarcity, the London's decorative female clerks also threatened disruption through the demand to have a good time, something not especially associated with either work or home. This contemporary quotation

**4.32** *Darling* (1965): Darling walks down the boardroom table.

refers to how the huge Lyceum ballroom in central London organised weekday lunchtime dancing sessions directed at office workers at the beginning of the 1960s:

> We used to wear very flared skirts with can-can petticoats underneath, and the more petticoats you had the better it was, so you'd be walking out dressed like someone on 'Come Dancing'. If anyone had tried to stop us wearing the clothes we would have changed our jobs . . . as soon as the lunch hour came round we would rush into the loo, get more petticoats on, backcomb the hair up another four inches, put the black lines on the eyes, fourteen-inch points on the feet and we'd be straight up the Lyceum. Jiving at the Lyceum was really the highlight of our day because the work that we were doing was so boring and this was the one thing that we really wanted to do . . . we might be ten or fifteen minutes late getting back to the office but usually no-one said anything.[44]

For a moment, the time was right to challenge David Harvey's 'single most important fact' about industrial capitalism: that 'it forced a separation between the place of work and the place of reproduction and consumption'. The made-up, decorative office girls suggest another, fun-loving, possibility.

## Notes

1    David Harvey, *Consciousness and the Urban Experience*, (Oxford: Blackwell, 1985), p. 37.

2    'Paris – the Capital of the Nineteenth Century' in Walter Benjamin, *Charles Baudelaire: A Lyric Poet in the Era of High Capitalism*, (London & New York: Verso, 1983), p. 155.

3    Ibid., p. 36.

4    *The Shorter Oxford English Dictionary*, 3rd edition (USA: Guild Publishing, 1983).

5    Benjamin, op. cit., p. 167 (also quoted in this book's Endpiece).

6    'With fingers busy at last, after long emancipation, they do "batik-work", "poker-work", "stencilling", "fretwork", "metalwork", "lampshade work", and any other work that can be devised.' John Betjeman, 'A Guide to the Recent History of Interior Decoration', in the *Architectural Review*, May 1930, quoted in Mary and Neville Ward, *Home in the Twenties and Thirties*, (UK: Ian Allan Ltd., 1978), p. 63.

7    Griselda Pollock, 'Modernity and the Spaces of Feminity', in *Vision and Difference: Feminity, Feminism and the Histories of Art*, (UK: Routledge, 1988), p. 67.

8    F.R. Yerbury, editor, *Modern Homes Illustrated*, (London: Odhams Press, 1948), p. vxvii.

9    See discussions in Chapters 1, 2 and 3.

10    Previously quoted in Chapter 2. Brian Finnimore, *Houses from the Factory: System Building and the Welfare State*, (London: Rivers Oram Press, 1989), p. 103.

11    This notion is extrapolated from Catherine Ingraham, 'Lines and Linearity Problems in Architectural Theory', in Andrea Kahn, *Drawing Building Text*, (USA: Princeton Architectural Press, 1991), p. 69.

12    Quoted in translation in Benjamin, op. cit., p. 45.

13    *Alfie* (UK: Paramount/Sheldrake, 1966), director, Lewis Gilbert.

14    See Chapter 3.

15    Alfie's own words.

16    Dennis Crompton, 'City Synthesis', The Living City (1963), article reproduced in *A Guide to Archigram 1961–74*, (London: Academy Editions, 1994), p. 88.

17    London Building Act of 1894, cited in S. Humphries and J. Taylor, *The Making of Modern London 1945–1985*, (London: Sidgwick & Jackson, 1986), p. 55.

18    In 1881 there were 7,000 women clerks in England and Wales. By the year 1911 there were 146,000: the Civil Service in 1914 employed 600 women; in 1920 170,000; in 1911 women constituted a quarter of all clerical workers; in 1951 there were 2,123,500 office workers: 845,700 were men and 1,277,800 women. Statistics taken from Alan Delgado, *The Enormous File: A Social History of the Office*, (London: John Murray, 1979), pp. 46, 121 and 93.

19    Margaret Dent, quoted in Humphries and Taylor, op. cit., p. 56.

20    See for example *The Architects' Journal*, 21 August 1968, p. 310, article on Seifert entitled 'Think Big': 'One can only assume that architect Colonel Seifert and his clients must have that questionable adage "Think big" hung over their beds . . .'

21    *The Seven Year Itch* (USA: TCF, 1955), directors, Charles K. Feldman, Billy Wilder.

22    Manhattan's share of the regions employment in accounting offices/commercial banks declined, but office employment grew by about 10 per cent between 1947 and 1956, from 753,000 to 830,000. Statistics taken from M. Edgar Hoover and Raymond Vernon, *Anatomy of a Metropolis*, (USA: Harvard UP, 1959) p. 93.

23    William R. Taylor, *In Pursuit of Gotham City: Culture and Commerce in New York*, (New York: Oxford University Press, 1992) p. 64.

24    *The Apartment* (USA: UA/Mirisch, 1960), director, Billy Wilder.

25    In 1956 311,700 office workers were employed in the financial community, 83,200 in life and health insurance statistics. From *Table 18: Distribution of Financial Community, New York Metropolitan Region, 1956*, in Edgar Hoover and Vernon, op. cit., p. 95.

26    Ibid., *Table 33: Specialization of Jobs and Residents by Counties of New York Metropolitan Region, 1950*, p. 158.

27    Ibid., p. 171.

28    The change occurs in less than a decade: charted in the difference between Helen Gurley-Brown, *Sex and the Single Girl*, (USA: NY Pocket, 1963) to *Nice Girls Do: 'Vanity Fair's' Guide to the New Sexual Etiquette*, (USA: Hearst, 1971).

**29**   See Chapter 3.

**30**   Nevertheless, *among women* it has been recognised that their role in the office has been fraught with sexual and social ambiguity from the outset. Alan Delgado quotes the American *Business Women's Journal* of 1889: 'Never accept gifts and other attention from your employer unless he has introduced you to members of his family and you have been received as a social equal of them', op. cit., Delgado, p. 45.

**31**   Ibid., pp. 54 and 56.

**32**   Val Hill, quoted in Humphries and Taylor, op. cit., p. 69.

**33**   Adrian Forty, *Objects of Desire: Design and Society 1750–1980*, (London: Thames & Hudson, 1986), p. 149.

**34**   Burt Bacharach, Hal David, *Wives & Lovers* (Famous Music/BMG Publishing Ltd).

**35**   Quoted from an advertisement for '*Charm*: the Magazine for Women who Work', Ellen Lupton, *Mechanical Brides: Women and Machines from Home to Office*, (USA: Princeton University Press, 1993), p. 54.

**36**   *A Guide for the Married Man* (USA: TCF, 1967), director: Frank McCarthy.

**37**   Humphries and Taylor, op. cit., pp. 68–9.

**38**   'Pains had been taken from early on to restrict extended individual one-to-one contact between senior management and clerical staff, via the imaginative use of available technology. An advertisement from the *K&J News* of October 1921 (Delgado, op. cit., p. 47), shows a spacious open plan typing pool with supervisor and notes: "Directors, Managers, Clerks, and others summon typists for dictation as required, by telephone communication with the supervisor, and are at all times free from the distracting noise of the machines." Thus the intimacy of the telephone was controlled and used to impose an even greater level of remoteness on the women in the typing pool. Objections were (continuously) made to the dictating machine on the grounds that it reduced this intimacy; its very attraction for management experts' (Forty, op. cit., p. 138).

**39**   Mary Haddock, 'Architects and their Offices', in *Building*, 10 February 1967.

**40**   The significance of upholstery is indicated in this passage in Benjamin op. cit., which refers explicitly to its responsiveness to the traces of life, in implicit contrast to the washable surfaces of modernism: 'The interior was not only the private citizen's universe, it was also his casing. Living means leaving traces. In the interior, these were stressed. Coverings and antimacassars, boxes and casings, were devised in abundance, in which the traces of everyday objects were moulded. The resident's own traces were also moulded in the interior', p. 169.

**41**   I am indebted to Peter Thornton for this information.

**42**   Adrian Forty, op. cit., p. 128.

**43**   *Sabrina* (US title) (USA: Paramount, 1954), director: Billy Wilder.

**44**   Anne Henderson, office worker, quoted in Humphries and Taylor, op. cit., pp. 67–8.

**Part three:** The City

## Chapter 5
## Free circulation = free copulation:
women and roads in *Nana* and *Two or Three Things I Know About Her*

> Ambiguity is the *figurative* appearance of the dialectic, the law of dialectic at a standstill. [emphasis added] This standstill is Utopia, and the dialectical image therefore a dream image. The commodity clearly provides such an image: as fetish. The arcades, which are both house and stars, provide such an image. And such an image is provided by the whore, who is seller and commodity in one.[1]

In the previous chapter, I suggested that the rift between home and work provoked a persistent dream of the post-war modernised city. The dream was of a place where the man could drift untrammelled by distinctions between inside and outside. Both metaphorically and literally this idea of the dissolution of the border has had its impact on the feminine. It has been felt on the interior of women's own bodies; on their inhabitation of the architectural interior both at home and at work; and on the cultural characterisation of women either as balm or irritant to the symptoms of this home/work division.

There is a curious parallel to these varying female personifications. It works at city scale in two fictions about Paris I discuss in this chapter. Emile Zola's novel *Nana*, was published in 1880, and set in the Paris of the 1860s. A hundred years separates the Paris described in Jean-Luc Godard's film *Two or Three Things I Know About Her*, released in the mid-1960s.[2] These two fictions have notable similarities which help to highlight the particular character of the contemporary urban expansion of their two versions of Paris.

The fictions of both these writers are part of a political project. Zola is a realist.[3] Ostensibly he uses his fiction to play out a scientific thesis on heredity: his heroine is overwhelmingly destructive despite herself, because of 'bad blood'. Godard, for the space of this film at any rate, explores the possibilities of structuralism: his heroine too, behaves in spite of her own individuality, and directly enacts the social and economic structures which define her. In both Godard's film and Zola's novel the construction of the city, in particular road construction, forms another metaphorical layer between the heroine and the over-arching structures of everyday reality.

In *Nana* and *Two or Three Things I Know About Her*, the 'Her' who is the 'heroine' refers self-consciously both to a prostitute, and, at one and the same time, to the city of Paris. Both are set in periods of intense turmoil. To read this novel and to see this film is to experience an assault on the accepted notion of Paris of a civilised and controllable city, and to find instead a place subject to the most naked effects of capitalist greed.

*Nana* takes place in 1867, just before the siege of Paris by Prussia, which was followed by the short-lived Paris Commune. The Commune was the first ever attempt to organise a large-scale society on recognisably Communist grounds. Godard's film deals with another pre-revolutionary moment: the then present day, 1967, the year before Paris was once more brought to a standstill by popular will, and there was for a moment a real possibility of organising an alternative to capitalist society. The moment came to be known as the May Events of 1968.

In both the 1960s' and the 1860s' fictions, Paris is ripped apart and reconstituted by major road building. The history of large-scale road building in Paris can be read very clearly as an accreting series of rings, which follow the lines of the series of walls encircling the city at various periods of its expansion. Moreover, the identification of road building with the defence of vested interests, is real, not just metaphorical. The road builders directly identify 'vested interests' with the Paris inside the walls. It seems that Parisian ring-road construction both follows periods of unrest and immediately heralds such periods as well. The construction of a wall with custom posts controlling entry and exit in the years just preceding 1798 is recognised as a major provocation of the Revolution.[4] In the 19th century, the huge project initiated by Baron Haussmann, referred to in the previous chapter, was a response to the Revolutions of 1848: and ironically provided the wherewithal for the possession of Paris by the Communards. This is the period of Zola's *Nana*.

In the second half of the 20th century the giant ring-road called the *Périphérique*, which now defines 'central' Paris, was under construction. This road deliberately isolated the sites of working-class occupation in the suburbs in a bid to sanitise the city centre, partly in response to the riots against the Algerian War of the early 1960s. As in previous attempts, the imposition of an excluding line appeared to acerbate the ferment it was intended to suppress. The newly built housing adjacent to the *Périphérique* is the setting for Godard's film.

In Zola's novel, Nana herself 'occupied the second floor of a large new house on the Boulevard Haussmann, whose landlord let flats to single ladies so that they should suffer the first inconveniences'.[5] Zola places Nana on the invasive boulevard which is directly identified with the ruthless road builder himself, and which leads to the new Opera House designed by Charles Garnier. It is in the process of completion: hence the reference to 'the first inconveniences'. The chaos involved in tearing the road open is vividly apparent in this contemporary image (Fig. 5.1).

**5.1** Building the Boulevard Haussmann.

The Opera House can be seen vaguely in the distance. Zola describes the scene experienced by Muffat, one of Nana's lover/victims:

> Day broke at last, that grey dawn that follows winter nights, and looks so melancholy from the muddy Paris pavements. Muffat had returned to the wide streets which were then being laid on either side of the new Opera. Soaked by the rain and broken up by cart-wheels, the chalky soil had turned into a quagmire.[6]

As in Polanski's *Repulsion*[7] the distinction between road and earth below has become blurred; the addition of rain adds further to the confusion between accepted lines of urban demarcation. The sorry state to which Nana has reduced Muffat, the once proud aristocrat, is conveyed by describing him as a victim of the road-building, his individuality subsumed by its obliterating power: he is 'constantly slipping and recovering his balance', people staring 'at him in surprise, struck by his soaked hat, his muddy clothes and his dazed expression'.[8]

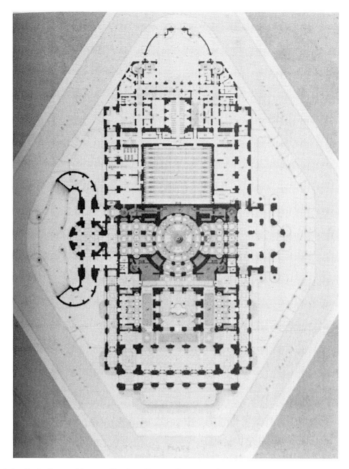

**5.2** Plan of the Paris Opera House, Charles Garnier (1861–74), indicating its interconnection with the road's axis.

The plan of Garnier's Opera House can be read in the light of *Nana* as an expression of the smearing of expected borders within the city. The plan, rendered in the Beaux Arts manner, suggests the boulevard invading and dematerialising the fabric of the building itself. Walls are virtually illegible; the building is almost like a pavilion constructed with columns, while the axis of the road becomes all-important (Fig. 5.2).

The plan then implies an entirely public space: a set of interior spaces shaping, but not interrupting or enclosing, the axis from the Boulevard Haussmann.

Unlike Nana, the 'Her' of *Two or Three Things I Know About Her*, is non-specific: she is personified by a number of different women. The nameless, generic

'She' lives just by the new *Périphérique*, which Godard depicts under construction. This renting of Paris by the 1960s' road scheme takes a radically different form from a century earlier. Instead of either dematerialising the buildings around it, or forcing acknowledgment through the imposition of uniform frontages of the road, the formal relationship set up by the *Périphérique* has no such reciprocity: it is one of absolute difference. This formal difference delineates and distinguishes the road as other from its surroundings.

Godard's *Périphérique* sweeps through the city at high level, ignoring the vertical spatial hierarchy of the buildings it cuts through, isolating them, and rendering them forlorn objects, subordinated to the road's curvaceous power (Fig. 5.3). The prostitute mouths lifelessly at the camera that she lives: 'in the big block near the Autoroute du Sud – you know: the big blue and white buildings' (Fig. 5.4).

For Godard, place has become recognisable solely in the most formulaic way: buildings can only be identified in the same manner that consumers distinguish between commodities. He makes this explicit in a shop scene where 'She' listlessly considers what clothes to buy. 'She' says, 'My sweater is blue, but what if blue had been called green by mistake?'. The sequence deliberately makes no distinction between these apparently vacuous considerations, and her musings on the future of the city which follow. She speaks in the same monotone, with the same abstracted gaze, never addressing the camera, as it were, in the eyes, and with the same image of her head filling the frame. She continues, 'No one knows what the future of the

5.3 *Two or Three Things I Know About Her* (1967): The *Périphérique* under construction.

**5.4** *Two or Three Things I Know About Her* (1967): 'You know: the big blue and white buildings'.

**5.5** *Two or Three Things I Know About Her* (1967): 'No one knows what the future of the city will be like.'

city will be like. Part of the wealth of meaning the city once had will undoubtedly be lost. The creative and formative roles of the city may be taken over by TV and radio' (Fig. 5.5).

'I go to Paris twice a month' says the prostitute who lives in the big blue and white buildings. The construction of the *Périphérique*, serving the purpose of capitalism, masquerading under the guise of benign planning, has commodified Paris itself. It has made Paris into a distinct and separate object, that Parisians themselves have to arrange to visit. Contemporary critics of the film noted how the aesthetic power of Godard's eye made the commodified world he criticised strangely seductive.[9] In urban terms at least, I would argue that this is quite self-conscious. As it turns out, this no-place with its own visual seductions is not a simple victim, a straightforward site of downfall with no power or impetus of its own.

The myth of the so-called May events in Paris focuses on the 'traditionally revolutionary' sites of central Paris: the prevailing sentimental image is of students and workers linking arms across the width of Haussmann's boulevards. But the cauldron of this short-lived revolutionary moment was Nanterre, a new-built Parisian suburb, indistinguishable from the no-place of Godard's film. Nanterre, too, is just the other side of the *Périphérique*; it is the site of a new university built in anonymous precast concrete blocks. In contrast to the central Parisian Sorbonne, a university precinct founded in the Middle Ages, and integrated into the urban fabric at the heart of the city, Nanterre itself exists as a separate object: a campus university. At the time dubbed a blueprint for the universities of the future, the left-wing critic Alain Touraine, who taught there himself, describes it: 'Nanterre is above all as a place, the opposite of Paris',[10] 'Neither beautiful nor ugly, its buildings respond to an image of what a faculty must be, if you accept a Fordist conception of the idea. They are conceived of as a production line; they guarantee good organisation of production flows.'[11] Nanterre is therefore the very essence of zoned specialisation, and repels the impurity of other potentially corrupting urban uses. Nanterre was a symbol of the massive expansion in university places in France from 123,000 in 1946 to 514,000 in 1968.[12] A contemporary description is reminiscent of Zola writing about the Boulevard Haussmann:

> Beyond the cheap housing which rings Nanterre is an industrial wasteland, shabby and scarred. There are railway sidings, the gaping trench of a planned express Metro, the gash of a new motorway under construction. Underfoot there is mud, and gravel and patches of sparse grass. Studies are pursued to the grinding of earth moving machines and the shunting of freight trains.[13]

Patrick Seale and Maureen McConville, two journalists writing at the time, themselves quote Alain Touraine, observing that 'the student campus isolates students in the way workers are isolated in "company towns"'. They understand this product of large-scale urban purification works to foment a new kind of class consciousness:

> The student crowd is born; as dense and faceless as an industrial proletariat with its own grievances, its own leaders and its growing sense of power.[14]

But the sense of Godard's film is not just that Paris has been atomised into objects: it is that it is decimated. Despite the ambiguities of his camera, the figure of the prostitute is first and foremost the victim of the ruthless practices of international capital, symbolic of the body of Paris, and indeed France herself.

As if her body were itself the subject of a vast engineering project, in a sequence of close-ups of her prone body draped in the red, white and blue of the French flag, she tells the camera that she has dreamt 'that I was being sucked into a huge hole' (Fig. 5.6), and feels 'as if I have been torn into a thousand pieces'. The very embodiment of Freudian condensation, 'She' is at one and the same time the whole of France, the specific site violated by the *Périphérique*, turned into a thousand objects, and the living figure of the prostitute/victim herself who inhabits the new Paris, where she is forced to live in the wrecked constituents of her own formerly coherent body. She inhabits the world of the block, where the road has rendered the buildings 'a thousand pieces'. 'She' herself, like the prefabricated buildings of chapter 4 (Figs 4.4 and 4.5) where inside is merely the reverse of outside, has no separate, individual interior. Filmed from within these Parisian prefabricated flats, the camera shows the prostitute's features wiped out. Even the limited individuality of her clothes is undistinguishable, requiring the commentator to inform the viewer that 'she is wearing a midnight blue sweater with two yellow stripes' (Fig. 5.7).

True to the prejudices of its times, the metaphor of the prostitute in *Nana* is used to suggest a perpetrator rather than a victim of destruction. For the most part the heroine Nana, and her double, the Haussmannian forces of modernisation, willingly engage in destructive rampage: eventually both are called to account for the havoc they have wreaked. For Zola, Nana is the active culprit associated with the ruthless upheaval of the road itself. The road is the figure: Paris is the ground destroyed by Nana's rampant sexuality, unequivocally linked with the uncontrollable power of early capitalism. The compelling, profoundly ambiguous combination of sophisticated eroticism and contemporary misogyny which drive this metaphor is overt in Zola's outline of the novel, written in 1878:

> a force of Nature, a ferment of destruction, but without meaning to, simply by means of her sex and her strong female odour, destroying everything she approaches, and

turning society sour just as women having a period turn milk sour. The cunt in all its power; the cunt on an altar, with all the men offering up sacrifices to it. The book has to be the poem of the cunt, and the moral will lie in the cunt turning everything sour . . . Nana eats up gold, swallows up every sort of wealth; the most extravagant tastes, the most frightful waste. She instinctively makes a rush for pleasures and possessions. Everything she devours; she eats up what people are earning around her in industry, on the stock exchange, in high positions, in everything that pays.[15]

If the path of the Haussmannian boulevard in *Nana* penetrates into buildings subordinating them to events in a public promenade, then Nana herself takes positive enjoyment in this new world of continuous circulation. This active engagement is suggested by the overtaking of the interior by the world of the exterior, with its plethora of diverse commodities.

She adored the Passage des Panoramas[16] . . . She could not tear herself away from the shop-windows . . . lost in wonder in front of a confectioner's wares, or listening to a musical-box in a neighbouring shop, and above all going into ecstasies over cheap, gaudy knick-knacks, such as nutshell work-boxes, rag pickers baskets for holding toothpicks and thermometers mounted on obelisks and Vendôme columns.[17]

The consumption of early capitalism provides Nana with a wealth of choice, a riot of possibility: in Godard's late version, global monopoly has reduced all this variety to the question 'have you got it in green or blue?'.

The 19th-century Parisian arcade allowed unimpeded access to infinite commodities, and unimpeded movement across the city, combined with the dissolution of the distinction between interior and exterior. As indicated in the previous chapter, for Walter Benjamin, the same forces forged the arcades and the separation between home and work. It was the separation of home and work which allowed the 19th-century interior its distinct character, as purveyor of illusion, literally cushioning its inhabitants from the unmediated forces of capitalist exploitation. In turning the dweller within into an anonymous silhouette, Godard's interior refuses point blank to support its inhabitants in their 'illusions' of individuality. In this way, his interior performs in the opposite manner to Benjamin's 19th-century softly cushioned 'complement' to the office. The interior of the new blocks is as transparent an operation of capitalism as the means of production themselves. This point is underlined by the repeated depiction by Godard of the kitchen as a production line for the home, where the housewife stands anonymously with her back to the interior space processing the household goods with the aid of prominently displayed, internationally branded commodities. These same commodities, ostensibly belonging

**5.6** *Two or Three Things I Know About Her* (1967): 'In my dreams I used to feel that I was being sucked into a huge hole.'

used to feel that I
into a huge hole

*She is wearing a midnight blue sweater with two yellow stripes*

**5.7** '*Two or Three Things I Know About Her* (1967): The mass-produced interior wipes out individuality: she is identified only by her clothing "a midnight blue sweater with two yellow stripes"'

to the interior, are set out in the careful architectural model of the new Paris of objects that is a parting shot of the film.

So, in *Two or Three Things I Know About Her*, at these blocks-without-interiors where 'She' lives, the road does not operate, as it does a hundred years earlier, to legitimate public circulation into formerly intimate parts of the city. As I've indicated, the road of Godard's film works like an avenging arm of international finance, making the blocks beyond the *Périphérique* random objects within a field. While the city blocks of Haussmann's Paris had to front, and formally acknowledge, the new boulevards through devices such as the regulation of uniform cornice heights, the blocks of the *Périphérique* and the road itself exist in apparent blind indifference one to the other. The paradox is that it is the very rendering of the new residential blocks as free-standing objects which promotes the dream of 'Libre circulation' – free movement – a student demand that was a spark to the May events.

The slogan 'Libre Circulation' – 'free movement', was an ultimatum that the final logic of the city of objects be conceded. The demand was for unimpeded access to women's bedrooms on university campuses: movement, as in the contemporary London film, *Alfie*, conceived of as an act allowing male penetration its inexorable ends. The male and female residential blocks of the new French campus universities were strictly segregated and guarded by warden's lodges. In the 'Red Autumn' of

1965, preceding the events of 1968, 1,700 students forcibly prevented builders from erecting a warden's lodge in front of a women's hostel in Antony, a southern suburb of Paris. In the spring of 1967 the demand for 'Libre Circulation' drove male students to invade the women's hostel at Nanterre, and to be removed by the police and fire brigade. This demand spread like wildfire in the early months of 1968: it was a rallying cry for students. At the universities of Nantes, Nice and Montpellier, further mass attempts were made to force this new kind of movement. The police were called in – and, at Montpellier, the students overpowered them. The underlying purport of this 'right' is revealed in contemporary accounts, which state that to the graffito 'Libre circulation' was appended the demand for 'Libre copulation' – unbridled copulation.[18] The contemporary picture at Nanterre is further complicated by the fact that numbers of prostitutes were living on campus. In a pre-eminently practical and successful assault on the rigid urban zoning of the new Paris, these women had registered as so-called 'phantom students': not to study, but for the room, the meals and the privileges of the student card. They were known as 'les Demoiselles de Nanterre'.[19]

In *Two or Three Things I know About Her*, Godard creates his own version of the Nanterre prostitutes' direct action. It involves some startling challenges to our habits of categorisation. Prostitutes' activities are generally only tolerated within extremely distinct time and space. In Godard's film this space is, as in medieval London, outside of the city walls, in the bland storage containers beyond the *Périphérique*. He emphasises, however, that they are wage earners for the family working in daylight hours. The consumers of this human commodity impose silence, or verbal aquiescence from the prostitutes themselves with whatever fantasy is required. The prostitutes of the Godard's film, though, regain their own voice, against this bought submission. When they appear at their most subordinated – i.e. in the midst of their wage-earning – they voice not the punters' fantasies, but, incongruously, the film's urban and philosophical commentaries. The way the subtitled version reveals this is disturbingly visual. The imagery of beautiful women doing as they are bidden works as a sexploitation movie – and entirely at odds with their exploratory discourse which speaks, in solidarity with their own personal, unspoken subjugation and resistance, of the subjugation and the resistance of the city itself to just the same forces of commodification.

In a scene where two prostitutes have been hired to service an American war photographer on leave from Vietnam, once again the camera obliterates the individuality of 'She'. She is placed in profile against a window. The contrasting commentary as 'She' takes off her clothes is of the parallel, elusive individuality of the city under threat, Paris herself. Here the 'She' that is both woman and city, allows Paris to be described in archetypically female terms: 'Paris is a mysterious city . . .

**5.8** *Two or Three Things I Know About Her* (1967): 'He enjoys it better if we don't look.'

if we don't look

**5.9** *Two or Three Things I Know About Her* (1967): Bags on their heads.

asphyxiating, natural'. The final, darkly comic, requirement of the photographer's fantasy compels the women to sacrifice their exteriors as well as sites for commodification. At this point the camera momentarily restores their individuality by revealing their faces, only to cover them again, this time with TWA and Pan Am flight bags (Figs. 5.8. and 5.9).

On the 18th March 1968 a student walked into the Right Bank of Paris and blew in the windows of Chase Manhattan, the Bank of America and Trans-World Airlines.[20] Together with the demand for 'Libre Circulation' it was acknowledged as a catalytic moment of the 1968 events.

Nana similarly assaults the established world. In her case, though, it is the aristocratic world of old money:

> Taken by a whim, she insisted on his [Muffat's] coming one evening dressed in his
> superb uniform of court chamberlain . . . Laughing all the time, and carried away by
> her irreverence for pomp and grandeur, and by the joy of humiliating him in the official
> dignity of his uniform, she shook him and pinched him, shouting: 'Get a move on,
> chamberlain!' and finally kicking him in the behind. Every kick was a heartfelt insult to
> the Tuileries and the majesty of the imperial court, dominating an abject and frightened
> people.[21]

Zola suggests the destruction of meaning via a maddened heightening of the senses: Godard, the destruction of meaning through the literally fetishising commodification of sex. In one Paris the road penetrates everywhere, making everything available to it and part of it. In the Paris of the 20th century, the road makes of every building an object, which the revolutionising male forces then demand that they have the right to penetrate. Like a consummate promiscuous flaneur, the new territory allows the revolutionary Don Juans to have their cake and eat it. This is *Alfie* with politics.

For Zola, Nana herself is the embodiment of rampant urban expansion, Paris running riot: literally swallowing up the virgin countryside:

> At every mouthful Nana swallowed an acre. The leaves quivering in the sunshine, the vast fields of ripe corn, the golden September vineyards, the tall grass in which the cows stood knee-deep – everything was engulfed as if in an abyss . . . Nana passed by like an invading army, or one of those swarms of locusts whose fiery flight lays waste a whole province. She scorched the earth on which her little foot rested.[22]

*Nana* threatens lack of delineation and definition, both of objects and of social entities. She destroys because she swallows up distinction, between aristocrat and prostitute, between city and countryside. But Paris, the mysterious asphyxiating 'She' of Godard's film, is the victim of the mission to delineate it and control it. In the context of this quotation from Nana, it is of particular interest that Godard refuses to accept the formulation of Paris in opposition to the 'nature' that surrounds it. At the end of his film, he contrasts two images of Paris as a whole. Paris the object is thrown wilfully on the grass 'without reference to the needs of eight million inhabitants' (Fig. 5.10). Paris the bunch of flowers is similarly cast down (Fig. 5.11). The bouquet spreads out at will, its edges far too intricate, interrelated and complex to ever draw a line around. Paris the flowers refuses its reduction to a simple opposition to its elusive background.

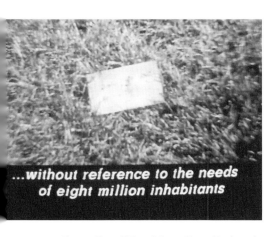

5.10 *Two or Three Things I Know About Her* (1967): Paris flung on the ground 'without reference to the needs of eight million inhabitants'.

5.11 *Two or Three Things I Know About Her* (1967): Paris as a bunch of flowers.

## Notes

1   *Charles Baudelaire: A Lyric Poet in the Era of High Capitalism*, (London & New York: Verso, 1983), p. 171.

2   *Two or Three Things I Know About Her* (France: Contemporary/Anouchka/Argos/Les Films de Carosse/Parc Film, 1967), director: Jean-Luc Godard.

3   The French realist school 'insisted on accurate documentation, sociological insight, an accumulation of the details of material fact . . . and subjects were to be taken from everyday life, preferably from lower-class life. This emphasis clearly reflected the interests of an increasingly positivist and scientific age.' *The Oxford Companion to English Literature*, edited by Margaret Drabble, (UK: Oxford University Press, 1998), p. 808.

4   George Rudé, *The Crowd in the French Revolution*, (UK: Oxford University Press, 1959).

5   Emile Zola, *Nana*, translation by George Holden, (London: Penguin, 1972), p. 22.

6   Ibid., p. 235.

7   See Chapter 3.

8   Zola, op. cit., p. 235.

9   'A creative personality at the height of its powers; combining all the disparate elements into a fascinating kaleidoscope showing familiar objects in new and arresting lights; against all his own intentions turning the world he deplores so much, the plastic consumer society of Paris, into a world of strange and wonderful forms', David Robinson, *The Financial Times*, sleeve notes, *Two or Three Things I Know About Her* (London, Conoisseur Video, 1992).

10   Alain Touraine, *Le Mouvement de Mai ou le Communisme Utopique*, (Paris: Editions du Seuil, 1968), pp. 97–8.

11   Ibid., p. 99: Touraine continues: 'Nevertheless I loved Nanterre from the first day I knew it . . . in its brutality, in its distance from the Latin Quarter, Nanterre was a sign of rupture with the Parisian university world. I didn't love it for what it was but for what it wasn't. Nanterre, by its very existence, was a critique of the idea of the University. In the same way as one can love brutal cities, where riches and misery clash together, without being masked by any historic patina, Nanterre revealed the University as it is, not as it appears to be through a religiously maintained hagiography', ibid., p. 101 (Author's translation). Note the continued use of the word 'brutal': it bears direct comparison with Peter Smithson's apologia for Brutalism in Chapter 1.

12   Patrick Seale and Maureen McConville, *French Revolution 1968*, (London: Heinemann/ Penguin, 1968), p. 22.

13   Ibid., p. 26.

14   Ibid., p. 25.

15   Zola, op. cit. (quoted in introduction by George Holden), pp. 12–13.

16    The Passage des Panoramas was one of the new pedestrian arcades which opened up and exposed the interior of the old fabric of Paris as a result of Haussmann's remodelling.

17    Zola, op. cit., p. 215.

18    Seale and McConville, op. cit., p. 29.

19    Seale and McConville, op. cit., p. 26. A more idealised view of succcessful transgression is provided by Henri Lefebvre, quoted in the Endpiece section 'Form and Politics'. 'During those days the dichotomies between activity and passivity, between private life and social life, between the demands of daily life and those of political life, between leisure and work and the places associated with them, between spoken and written language, between action and knowledge, all these dichotomies disappeared in the *streets, amphitheatres and factories* [emphasis added] . . . Horrified and impotent, the adherents of norms witness the sequence of transgressions. They are unable to conceive of the initial transgression: the crossing of the border that "normally" separates the political and non-political areas, and the ensuing emancipation.'

20    Roger Absalom, *France: The May Events 1968*, (London: Longman, 1971), p. 4; Seale and McConville, op. cit., p. 19.

21    Zola, op. cit., p. 442.

22    Zola, op. cit., p. 436.

Chapter 6
**Against the city of objects:**
*Our Mutual Friend, Mary Poppins, L.A. Story*

Euclidean space . . . is literally flattened out, confined to a surface . . . The person who sees and knows only how to see, the person who draws and knows only how to put marks on a sheet of paper, the person who drives around and knows only how to drive a car – all contribute in their way to the mutilation of a space which is everywhere sliced up . . . the driver is concerned only with steering himself to his destination and in looking about sees only what he needs to see for that purpose; he thus perceives only his route, which has been materialised, mechanised and technicised and he sees it from one angle only – that of its functionality: speed, readability, facility . . . The reading of space that has been manufactured with readability in mind amounts to a sort of pleonasm, that of a 'pure' and illusory transparency. Space is defined in this context in terms of the perception of an *abstract subject*, such as the driver of a motor vehicle, equipped with a collective common sense, namely the capacity to read the symbols of the highway code, and with a sole organ – the eye – placed in the service of his movement within the visual field. Thus, space appears solely in its reduced forms. Volume leaves the field to surface and any overall view surrenders to visual signals spaced out along fixed trajectories already laid down in the 'plan'. An extraordinary – indeed unthinkable, impossible – confusion gradually arises between space and surface, with the latter determining a spatial abstraction which it endows with a half-imaginary, half-real physical existence. This abstract space eventually becomes the simulacrum of a full space . . . Travelling – walking or strolling about – becomes an actually experienced, gestural simulation of the formerly urban activity of encounter, of movement amongst concrete existences.[1]

The argument of this book has been that architecture plays out formal manifestations of pollution taboos, and that these manifestations both veil the operations of capitalism and coincide by and large with its interests. The fictions of film and the novel I have looked at have been used to unravel another story. In the context of the city, the over-riding idea of *defence of the border* means the question arises whenever a new demarcation or containment is made, what and who are being excluded? The original post-war forms of urban zoning have been roundly condemned in favour of 'mixed use'. But if we see zoning merely as one among *many* manifestations of the specialisation and commodification of urban space, then the apparently benign demarcations of borders – of conservation areas, housing action areas and pedestrianised zones – need all be questioned. This final chapter looks at alternative ways to envision the city, in particular, London, that fiction might bring.

In *Two or Three Things I Know About Her*, post-war Paris parallels a zoned London of single uses, conceived in contrast to its surroundings – the rest of Paris arbitrarily excluded by the giant ring-road, the *Périphérique*. Paris is a place in opposition to itself: the city's *alter ego*, the prostitute, says 'I feel as if I have been torn into a thousand pieces'. The planners', politicians' and capitalists' city forces an unnatural opposition: between Paris inside, and beyond, the border. On the other side of the line drawn by the road, Parisian urban zoning is starkly visible in the residential blocks, built for exclusively working-class and/or immigrant populations. Planned Paris is a city of specialised objects, set within a field, whose disquieting role is revealed in the film's model of a Paris made up of global commodities.

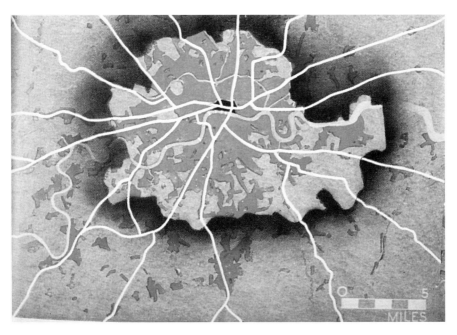

**6.1** *The County of London Plan* (1945) explained by E.J. Carter and Ernö Goldfinger: the uncontrolled spread of London as Red Peril.

Chapter 1 explored how the popular version of the 1944 plan for London shows the growth of the city as a 'red peril', threatening to take over South East England (Fig. 6.1). The fear of being overcome by something alien that the image projects is the wherewithal for support for the Green Belt, the ring of open country surrounding London, imposed as a result of the plan's adoption. Despite the declared intentions of the Green Belt, as an act of exclusion it puts a premium on the protected land, to the detriment of the inner city. The photographs in the Goldfinger version of the plan reveal that behind the imposition of this border is the sense of dirt which must contained in its place, and that place is in the inner city (Fig. 6.2).

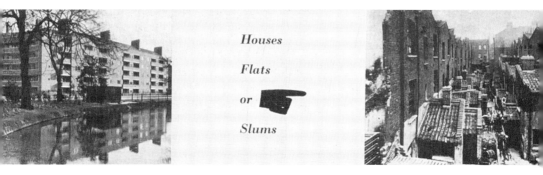

Houses

Flats

or

Slums

**6.2** *The County of London Plan* (1945) explained by E.J. Carter and Ernö Goldfinger: The inner city.

In Chapter 1, Fig 1.8, the plan's front cover, shows London as an island in a sea, complete with its own set of white cliffs. Centre and periphery are not just differentiated by an edge, they are fundamentally opposed types, land and sea. The possibility of mixing land and sea threatens the unordered chaos of drowning: the edge between the two must clearly be maintained at all costs. The undeniable clarity of this image and the content of the plan captured not just the official, but also the popular imagination of the time. This was the last time there was a plan for London you could actually see; if you were a local planner, you could literally hang it on the wall and it would tell you in broad outline, what to do, where. Numerous attempts at revision occurred in the post-war years, in particular a largely written plan, the Greater London Development Plan, in the 1970s. Nothing, though, was able to revise the devastating clarity and popular appeal of the original.

Richard Rogers wrote his book *A New London* with Mark Fisher at the beginning of the 1990s.[2] He continued the theme of containment akin to the Parisian and the Abercrombie model, to underline the distinction between centre and periphery (Fig. 6.3).

This model of opposition between the inside and outside of delineated areas continued to direct ideas of London's future – even in the dying years of Britain's Conservative government. The centre/periphery model, for example, is accepted in the *Strategic Guidance*[3] document issued in 1996. However, the imposition of large-scale planning *à la* Abercrombie was at odds with governmental free market principles. But at an architectural scale, a 1990s' version of zoning persisted. Large cultural

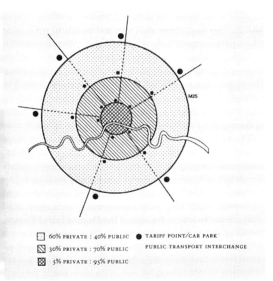

6.4 *Architects' Journal* (1999): A model of Sir Norman Foster's Greater London Assembly building.

60% PRIVATE : 40% PUBLIC   ● TARIFF POINT/CAR PARK
30% PRIVATE : 70% PUBLIC   PUBLIC TRANSPORT INTERCHANGE
5% PRIVATE : 95% PUBLIC

6.3 *A New London* (1992): Diagram of centre and periphery.

buildings were financed with money from a newly successful state-funded lottery. In effect, it put a state initiative on single-use constructions into effect. Buildings gaining government support were objects, formally legible as distinct from their surroundings, sticking out from their physical context. This applied not just to the biggest of these, the Millennium Dome, but also to Foster's Greater London Assembly building project (Fig. 6.4), and the Tate Modern, converted from a defunct riverside power station. The mind-set of saleability had in effect commodified the buildings: distinctions had to be as obvious and unmistakable as those between brands. Godard's grim depiction of this mind-set in his model of Paris as a set of commodities became so pervasive that even the new Assembly building became framed – presumably unnecessarily – in visual terms which declared that it could be immediately 'saleable' to the people.

The surrounding areas have been habitually objectified as well, distinguishing them from their untouched context. The Dome has its accompanying 'Millennium Village', while both the Assembly and Bankside buildings are situated in areas singled out for special planning treatment. Together with the universal adoption of conservation areas, numbers of planning edges have effectively objectified museum London to be cherished and encouraged, from rubbish London – the other side of the planners' border. In two ways London became conceived as a city of containment, of objects.

## Hollywood and the commodification of the city

Surrogate support for the city of objects emanates firmly from Hollywood. In the same way that museum London is contrasted with other London, each time Hollywood depicts Paris, London or New York, they are presented, by implication, in ossified contrast with Los Angeles. Hollywood visits these other cities in the form of familiar, oft-repeated objects, usually introduced from the air: the Manhattan skyline; the Eiffel Tower, closely followed by Sacré Cœur or Notre Dame; Big Ben, St Paul's Cathedral and the Tower of London.

Filmic Los Angeles, on the other hand is never objectified. There is no object that sums it up, despite the seedy hillside sign which literally spells out 'Hollywood'. It is implicitly accepted that Los Angeles is amorphous, ungraspable and impossible to see as an object from above. In reality, of course, the same applies to the London and Paris regions. But Hollywood's aerial views of Paris itself accept the lie of the tourist map: that is, that the *Périphérique* is like a moat around the city, and that what is beyond it is something else (Fig. 6.5).

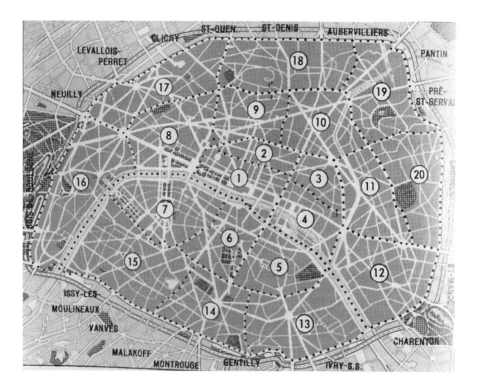

**6.5** Tourist map of Paris.

The equivalent descent on London, most famously depicted by Mary Poppins,[4] involves a far more thorough going doctoring: every part of London that is not deemed a recognisable object is swathed in a useful fog (Fig. 6.6).

**6.6** *Mary Poppins* (1964): Mary Poppins' descent on London.

Through the mist emerges Hollywood's judgement on what are London's big four: the Houses of Parliament, St Paul's, the Tower of London and Tower Bridge. Mary Poppins' London uncannily re-emerged as a prevailing image on the cover of the 1996 *Strategic Guidance* (Fig. 6.7). In both, London is done away with in favour of the same familiar lumps of tourist hardware.

As I've indicated, large-scale executive planning power was circumscribed by the favoured free-market ideology at the time of the *Strategic Guidance*'s publication. One of the only areas where it gave categorical direction was with regard to the objects depicted on its cover. Ten strategic views were identified from St Paul's Cathedral and the Palace of Westminster,[5] to be defended under legislation already in place. As in *Mary Poppins*, the unprivileged London-in-between could be understood as an undifferentiated mist (Fig. 6.8).

**6.7** *Mary Poppins* (1964): Skyline of London.

6.8 *Strategic Guidance for London Planning Authorities* (1995): Detail of front cover.

*Strategic Guidance for London Planning Authorities*

*Consultation Draft*

## Ealing and the city of objects

The embodiment of a city in an object is a theme of *The Lavender Hill Mob*,[6] like *Passport to Pimlico*,[7] another successful Ealing comedy of the immediate post-war period. By the 1940s it was established that the gangster mob in cinema exist in recognisably distinct urban places: they are depicted in the centre of cities, Chicago or New York. The genre distinguishes between mobsters and ordinary law-abiding people by placing the mob away from the blandly undistinguished suburbs of ordinary life. But Lavender Hill, a residential area of south west London, has just that bland suburban anonymity of the non-mobster.

What distinguishes Lavender Hill is not its physical, or indeed social form, but the eccentricities of the inhabitants. The comic contrast is between the nondescript architectural and physical clothing of the characters, and their original, dastardly inventiveness. These are master criminals who live an archetypal uneventful suburban life, habitually lodging with landladies, the recognised guardians of all aspects of post-war respectability.

The mob's plan is to import solid gold from Paris to replace the usual lead that lies hidden under the surface of gilt in souvenir models of the Eiffel Tower (Fig. 6.9). The ramification is that the success of their plot depends on the acceptance of Hollywood's cinematic view of both Paris and London as reducible to objects, legible at face value. The Lavender Hill mobsters exploit the space which is officially unrecognised, the space beneath the gilt is hidden away from, and does not contribute to, its familiar outline that Hollywood's terms signifies 'Paris'.

**6.9** *The Lavender Hill Mob* (1948): Alec Guinness discovers the hidden potential of the Eiffel Tower.

The Lavender Hill mob's lived experience of London acknowledges that just because a part of the city is *undelineated*, does not mean it does not exist. It is this knowledge that allows them to recognise the hidden form of the Eiffel Tower, the official encapsulation of the whole of Paris, as a usable space. True to their Lavender Hill understanding of the city, the mobsters don't buy into the city of iconic objects, but instead subvert it to their own hidden ends.

## Cinematic alternatives to the city of objects: Urban Hardware as friend

The London depicted in the *Lavender Hill Mob* is undifferentiated except by roads, and given distinct identity only by its inhabitants, those in the know. By its monuments you shall never know it. This dictum applies as well to Los Angeles, a city, perversely, *identifiable* through its absence of formal delineation, and, ironically home to Hollywood, the most determined purveyor of the city of objects. The early 1990s' comedy *L.A. Story*[8] starring Steve Martin, carries a complexity in its urban attitudes comparable to Ealing films about London. Like *The Lavender Hill Mob* it takes a rise out of cinema's habitual encapsulation of the city as an iconic object. In a kind of double irony, *L.A. Story* replicates the first shots of Fellini's *La Dolce Vita*.[9] *La Dolce Vita* depicts the glamorous life of the cinema crowd in Rome at the end of the 1950s. Each scene is framed by recognisable architectural icons: St Peter's, the Trevi Fountain, the Fascist-built suburb EUR. The film opens with an aeroplane circling over modern-day Rome which carries a graphic representation of Christ on the Cross, and is greeted variously by waving children and women in bikinis. In *L.A. Story* an equivalent plane waves a Big Hot Dog at the indifferent inhabitants below, and neatly incorporates a sideways swipe at New York's advertising promotion of itself as a Big Apple in the 1970s.

The impossibility of replicating a view of L.A. in a cinematic tradition of identifiable architectural objects is played with in the film's introductory sequence. It presents L.A. as a series of signs: a stream of identical men leap into a cloudless morning from a row of identical suburban houses, across identical lawns, and identical sprinklers spring into synchronised action; people with Christmas trees in bright sunshine; wearing gas masks against smog. Throughout the film L.A. has to be recognised not through its objects alone but by the degree to which they and their inhabitation reveal 'L.A.-ness'. Thus Martin is accosted by a mugger outside a fashionable new restaurant who introduces himself by saying 'Hi . . . I'm your mugger for this evening', and who at the end of the transaction tells him to 'have a nice day'.

The hero of *L.A. Story*, played by Martin, is Harris Telemacher, a hapless TV weatherman, frustrated by the total absence of weather variety in Los Angeles. Each cloudless day merges seamlessly into the next. This lack of discernible edges between experiences colours every situation in which he finds himself: endless alfresco dinner parties; constant forays down interchangeable motorways; houses, like his own, where the interiors are neither identifiable nor personalised. Strangely, given that this is a city known for the paucity of its public space, for Telemacher there is nowhere he can escape his public face: the city's requirement of him to be inanely happy.

**6.10**  *L.A. Story* (1991): A motorway sign demands 'sing doo wah diddy'.

Martin's moment of solace occurs on the hard shoulder of the motorway. A large electronic signpost suddenly interrupts its anonymous messages to drivers to demand that Martin hug it, and 'sing doo wah diddy' (Fig. 6.10).[10]

The signpost goes on to acquire an individual voice of humanity: a specific voice effectively expressed to the full scope of its admittedly rather limited architecture – larger writing, repetition and flashing. A piece of architectural hardware which everywhere else on the planet has only a generalised utilitarian value, in Los Angeles becomes almost painfully specific, familiar and a friend. Through a series of riddles it guides Telemacher to the film's conclusion: that you can find 'romance, deep in the heart of L.A.'.

Both London and Los Angeles are formally elusive, ungraspable. Harris Telemacher's inability to separate his sense of himself from his seamless context, in which the car, the dinner party, the TV studio, are indistinguishable, and his growing sense of panic, are the urban equivalent of Sartre's description of the experience of stickiness: 'a trap, it clings like a leech, it attacks the boundary between myself and it': touching L.A., Telemacher risks 'diluting himself into viscosity'.[11] The establishment of a physical touchstone within the city with whom he can converse, certain of a very peculiar difference and indeed whom he can hug, without compromising his own edges, allows the weatherman back his autonomy. Yet the mercurial quality of L.A. is also what enables Telemacher to find 'romance deep within it'. The built version of L.A. which appeals unashamedly to fantasy and fiction is ambiguous. When Telemacher is engaged in the most meaningless of sexual encounters L.A. is overtly a painted backdrop, through which he drifts in the manner of one in ordinary clothes walking behind the scenes on a film lot. Having kissed the right woman under direction of the signpost, a fictional garden is transformed into an entirely magical hyper-reality (Fig. 6.11).

**6.11** *L.A. Story* (1991): A fictional garden deep in the heart of L.A.

## The Familiar Writ Large – the city of characters

In both the film and book of *Mary Poppins*, Mary arrives in a world lacking structure and edges. The parents are manifestly incapable of keeping order in their household, and the children, without anyone to look after them, run wild. Mary arrives and imposes nursery convention with an iron will. But the enduring seductiveness of Mary Poppins rests on her ability to hold two contradictory roles at one and the same time. She presides over a topsy-turvy world outside the house, the existence of which she fiercely and categorically denies within it. What is more apparent within the book than in the film is that London is the amorphous world onto which she imposes her sites of external adventure. As in *L.A. Story*, Mary brings a system of larger-than-life friends into the city's anonymity – the multiple equivalents of Harris's motorway sign.

The map in *Mary Poppins in the Park*[12] both squares off London like a flat-worlder's map, and makes personalities both geographically fixed and of an equal status with monuments (Fig. 6.12).

Routes in London have no overt coherence: that is, unlike Paris or Manhattan, there is no overall plan, and the interconnectedness of networks across the city has no discernible intent or meaning behind it. Mary provides this meaning through her network of characters who, when experienced, loom even larger than the architectural monuments which in her world become their backdrops. The bird-seed seller who perpetually sits outside St Paul's Cathedral, presides over the whole of the City of London's life, like a nurse-maid, both night and day. She is never off duty and never 'goes home' any more than St Paul's itself (Fig. 6.13).

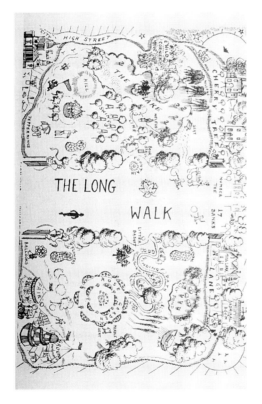

**6.13** *Mary Poppins* (1965): The Bird Lady outside St Paul's Cathedral.

**6.12** *Mary Poppins in the Park*: Mary Poppins' London.

If London as depicted in *The Lavender Hill Mob*, is self-consciously a world without monuments, site-specific only by virtue of the peculiar character of its inhabitants, then in P.L. Travers' version of London, monuments are characters writ large.

One interpretation of Mary Poppins in her role of cartographer, as much as nanny, is that through the judicious placement of that which is larger-than-life, she establishes a dual sense of excitement and security in our experience of the city. This sense of the city as a shapeless sea to be navigated, not by comprehensible networks, but by islands of safe familiarity is manifest in the aggressive marketing of new developments to the east of London in the old Docks areas in the early 1990s. It is noticeable from the 1980s onwards, when large-scale private residential development in this area first took off, that great play was made of the existing water as an element which positively isolated new residential accommodation, as if they were islands (Fig. 6.14).

More generally, selling Docklands was about isolated, contained experiences, all of which referred to the safety of the interior: already, by definition, contained and enclosed. Modernity is rarely overtly referred to, despite the manifest fact that Docklands was almost an entirely new development within London. Instead, what are encapsulated in window-like snapshots are the accustomed depictions of 'heritage' and 'tradition'. The Docklands publicity played a Mary Poppins-like game of duality: promoting the implicit excitement of the uncharted and unknown, and the safety of the familiar, but it reversed the intent. In the home Mary Poppins embodies

**6.14** Advertisement for Ideal Homes (1990): 'The Lakes' – water-bound housing in the redeveloped London Docklands.

**6.15**  Advertisement for Regalian, property developers (1990): Safe, character-free islands of 'Docklands Living'.

convention; in London-at-large, she calls on the unique and the outlandish to become landmarks in the otherwise undifferentiated scape. In the insecure London sea, the advertisements for Docklands frame familiar anonymity, explicitly character-free, and un-specific – with no surprises (Fig. 6.15).

## Networks of connection and networks of characters

A more complex use of characterisation as a tool for comprehending the city is a key theme of *The Chain*,[13] a mid-1980s' comedy about moving house in London. The film's structure layers a number of metaphors on top of one another. It deals with seven households moving into each other's properties across seven districts of London. Each character personifies both a district and one of the seven deadly sins: it is left to the viewer to decide how far the district itself as well as the character manifests the particular sin in question. The 'chain' in the title refers to a notorious feature of house purchase in England. It is impossible to move unless the person into whose home you are moving moves into another home, where someone else is waiting for another victim of the 'chain' to move from another home – and so on. The film assumes a model for London of formally unconnected areas; it uses the fact of the characters having to move, and each using the same removal firm as the sole physical link between the districts. The financial advantage, which is the unspoken link (in the film as in everyday life) precipitating removal, reveals the city's hierarchy of social class by district, directly expressed in London in the pricing of residential properties for sale. The film draws an arc from east to west London, describing an intricate scale of increasing money and increasing subtleties of social distinction. Like *The Lavender Hill Mob*, *The Chain* deliberately plays off the sense of London as an undifferentiated mass – to those uninitiated in the subtleties of distinction within the apparent sameness of London residences, each house in the chain appears much like another. The specificity is in the character, race and class of its inhabitants: histrionic Greek widow, dying Jewish tycoon, two minutely observed versions of the tight-arsed middle class, middle-middle and upper-middle, variously personifying Hammersmith, an aspiring upper-middle district, and Knightsbridge, an area of arrivistes.

The urban model of *The Chain* is a London without a centre and without formal links. Instead London is understood solely as a network of interconnections and, importantly, interdependencies. The parts of the London chain – Hackney, working class, Kilburn, lower-middle, and Knightsbridge, upper-middle, are explicitly revealed as equal and all subject to the various human failings expressed by the Deadly Sins – but different. Their specificity is scarcely formal, although the houses get further removed from the pavement using devices such as porticos, basements, front steps, as they increase in expense. However, *The Chain* heralds a new London to be understood and enjoyed: one where networks of ethnic multiplicity and absolute distinctness of character contrast poignantly both the apparent absence of delineation, and the absence of a centre in the city's external form.

## The river: absent and unfixed centre

The idea that the centre of London is absent is taken up in Doris Lessing's 1960s' novel *The Four Gated City*.[14] Her South African heroine, Martha Quest, finally reaches London just after the second world war. She seeks in vain for London's physical centre. She asks a bus conductor to tell her where Piccadilly Circus is:

> She looked at the haphazard insignificance of it, and the babyish statue, and began to laugh.
> 'My dear Martha?'
> 'This', she tried to explain, 'is the hub of the Empire.'[15]

This begins to suggest a London to be understood by its absences: the slightly sinister absence of an acknowledged centre of imperial power. Rasmussen's *London*,

*The Unique City* reminds us that even during the Middle Ages when London was pre-eminently graspable and containable, it had dual centres.[16] To the west, Westminster, the seat of royal influence, and to the east, the so-called 'City' of London, seat of financial power. It seems that from the start an identifiable, singular core of power was elusive. At the end of the 1980s, rioters chose the West End to vent their frustration with a tax on the poor;[17] at the end of the 1990s anti-capitalism campaigners ran riot in the City. On both occasions the West End and then the City remained uncannily untouched by any awareness of disturbance in the other part.

Martha's experience of London – 'In a street full of strangers, on the top of a bus in a part of London all barren little houses and smoking chimneys – who was she?',[18] – reiterates the sense of amorphous sameness of *The Lavender Hill Mob* and *The Chain*. She finally comprehends her own notion of centre:

> . . . by the river, looking down at the moving water, she was connected still with – a feeling of being herself. She was able to see herself as if from a hundred yards up, a tiny coloured blob, among other blobs, on top of a bus, or in a street. Today she could see herself, a black blob, in Mrs. Van's coat, a small black blob beside a long grey parapet. A tiny entity among swarms: then down, back inside herself, to stand, arms on damp concrete: this was what she was, a taste or flavour of existence without a name.[19]

The odd thing about a river as a 'centre' of an already uncontainable, undelineated city, is that the river is also by its nature just that: uncontainable and undelineated. It is literally unfixed and never the same. In the 1960s' film *Four in the Morning*,[20] the river performs an analagous role as kind of centre. The action of this film all takes place in or around the river – no man's land – and in no man's time, four o'clock in the morning. Two parallel narratives connect only because they take place at the same time of day in London, which is represented within both primarily as the river. The sense of absence of both the time and the landmarks signifying familiar views of place gives the film a backdrop against which the action is starkly written. The assertion of *Four in the Morning* seems to be that if the river is read as kernel of the city's life, it is not just physically unfixed, but unfixed in meaning. Time and place in the film contrast with urbanism's official urban version of what is substantial, and what is important. The river is introduced at the beginning of the film in just the same way as Hitchcock's *Frenzy* and Dickens' *Our Mutual Friend*, in the guise of murderer, or accomplice to a murder, with a drowned and nameless body hauled out from its depths.[21] Later, it is an unofficial playground for a newly met couple: they leap over the containing embankments and commandeer a speedboat. They are able to traverse London entirely freely, swooping back and forth, unrestricted by lines or routes, in

**6.16** *Four in the Morning* (1965): The river as ultra-modernist space.

a kind of ultra-modernist space (Fig. 6.16). The core of *Four in the Morning* London is entirely unofficial. It is uncategorised: neither road, square, building, house, nor park. The sense is that the speedboat charts the very heart of the city for the very first time. The river suddenly, unpredictably, reveals itself working as a formal centre: looking from its own centre, the monumental buildings of London are presented anew, and subordinated to the stature of the couple below (Fig. 6.17). This is possible, though, only by virtue of their unorthodox occupation of the river's space: their speed, which takes in huge swathes of vista all at once, and the ability of their boat to instantly ford the width of the river from Northbank to Southbank.

The couple's foray on the speedboat allows them an unusually prolonged occupation of the centre of this strangely fluid version of the city. Their adventures reveal what for the rest of us is ordinarily only instantaneous, always partial. This is the moment when crossing a bridge allows us, as it were, to *dwell* at the centre of the river. It is worth noting, however, that even these brief moments have inspired poets like William Wordsworth and Ray Davies to speculate on the nature of London as a whole.[22]

An understanding of the river as an unofficial centre, or at least a mechanism that links London experience in common, underlay planning policy at the end of the century. The Tory-commissioned *Strategic Planning Guidance for the River Thames*[23] arose from themes introduced in the more general *Strategic Guidance*. It suggests a growth in river transportation, a network of river centres, a continuous pedestrian access along the river edge. Yet the immense disagreements over the popular perception of this absent centre were lyrically revealed in the mid-1990s, at one of the mass debates concerning the future of London initiated by the Architecture Foundation. Voices were heard in loud protest at any attempt to tame or bind or contain the river – in particular by damming – or to smooth and make more urban its edges. There was an appreciation of a rough force which ploughed through the city, determining its own course despite all the various agendas seeking to incorporate

**6.17** *Four in the Morning* (1965): Tower Bridge seen from the centre of the river.

it in their own particular vision.[24] In particular its ambiguity, powerfully revealed in *Four in the Morning*, its continual change in character, was dwelt on.

## The city as mutual friend: networks of interconnection and the river

The fictions I've described indicate two antidotes to London circumscribed, or London ungraspable. Both the network of interconnection and the River Thames, a moving and changing centre, are overlaid as means to comprehend the city in Charles Dickens' last great book, *Our Mutual Friend*.[25] Like much of his work, *Our Mutual Friend* can be read as a novel in which the main character is London itself. The complexities of the book's structure allow a characterisation of London as a series of isolated figures who engage, as in *The Chain*, in a dialectical imprinting of their particular quirks on their locality and vice-versa. But the structure also allows the reverse: a comprehension of London as a network of interest and destiny, the elusive 'Mutual Friend' which links the separate characters. The reader who embarks on this vast narrative is, for the duration, a Londoner. The experience of reading the book replicates the experience of the city as a place without structure, meaning or centre. New narrative after new narrative is introduced with each chapter, without any apparent connection until well into this long book. So where we might expect a core, a reason for the novel, we find absence. In reading the novel we become detectives, we attempt to decipher, to find London.

Like *The Chain*, each new narrative immediately introduces a new individual and a new area of distinct character, and, also like *The Chain*, a particular moral standpoint. But this is emphatically not panoramic. In panorama London like Los Angeles doesn't work: it has no edges and no form. Everything is hidden within the townscape of *Our Mutual Friend*, or is not what it seems. Only one form does literally stick up like an object in the undifferentiated physical mass, and that is the mounds of filth and garbage which are the source of money, whose pursuit and rejection are one of the novel's themes. These objects reveal to the reader the material consequences of an urban view which prioritises money making over every other pursuit of the city. As for another representative of capitalism he describes, Mr Gradgrind in *Hard Times*, for Dickens the consequences of such materialism are a world view recognisable by the way reality is categorised into its 'original' elements.[26] For the businessman Podsnap in *Our Mutual Friend*, this reductivist approach is projected both onto the 'City' of London, the financial centre with St Paul's Cathedral at its heart, and onto all the arts. It enables him to confidently flourish away all else:

> Mr. Podsnap's world was not a very large world, morally; no, nor even geographically
> . . . Mr. Podsnap's notions of the Arts in their integrity might have been stated thus.

Literature; large print, respectively descriptive of getting up at eight, shaving close at a quarter-past, breakfasting at nine, going to the City at ten, coming home at half-past five, and dining at seven. Painting and sculpture; models and portraits representing professors of getting up at eight, shaving close at a quarter-past, breakfasting at nine, going to the City at ten, coming home at half-past five and dining at seven.[27]

The river itself in various guises runs through the many different lives of the novel. As in *Four in the Morning*, it is its ambiguity that paradoxically gives it the power to make a comprehensible link between events, people and places. At the beginning of the book it is as unequivocally degraded and filthy as the mounds of dirt. The heroine's father makes his living from robbing dead bodies he drags up. Dickens tells us that the river changes character vertically as well as horizontally. Father and daughter are 'allied to the bottom of the river rather than the surface by reason of the slime and ooze' with which their boat is covered. But it is also 'meat and drink'[28] and its driftwood is the source of the cradle that rocked the heroine to sleep when she was a baby.

If 'our mutual friend' is London in the guise of an elusive character crossing the book's several narratives, then the novel effectively begins with London's death. It is the body of 'our mutual friend', the character John Harmon, that has apparently been recovered from the Thames. The abiding quality of the river is its very elusiveness: and Dickens describes the social reaction to the Harmon murder as if that, too, were a river:

> Thus, like the tides on which it had been borne to the knowledge of men, the Harmon Murder . . . went up and down, and ebbed and flowed, now in the town, now in the country, now among palaces, now among hovels, now among lords and ladies and gentlefolks, now among labourers and hammerers and ballast-heavers, until at last after a long interval of slack water, it got out to sea and drifted away.[29]

The river is the source of redemption of two of the characters, and the nemesis of three others. The character 'our mutual friend', destined to inherit the mounds, has faked his own drowning: he is enabled to view his own death, his own physical dematerialisation – his putative body lying on a slab for identification – and his social dematerialisation. He is set free from classification by the fluidity of the river. It is through its squalid repulsiveness that he is reborn as John Rokesmith, and is able to turn the filthy lucre of the mounds of dirt to positive ends. Literally and figuratively, the power of the river, like London itself, is maintained through remaining a place which defies delineation and classification, both distinct and ungraspable.

In *Wuthering Heights*, Cathy, dreaming, wakes up from a dream within a dream. She is sobbing with relief. Instead of being in an ideal heaven, she finds herself here, on the grey earth. It is possible that our epoch's best dream of the future yet-to-come may involve, more than anything, a new conception of what we already have, but don't yet know.

## Notes

1   Henri Lefebvre, *The Production of Space*, (Oxford: Blackwell, 1991), p. 313.

2   Richard Rogers and Mark Fisher, *A New London*, (London: Penguin, 1992).

3   Government Office for London, *Strategic Guidance for London Planning Authorities: Consultation Draft*, (London: HMSO, 1995), pp. 8–9.

4   *Mary Poppins* (USA: Walt Disney, 1964), director: Robert Stevenson.

5   *Strategic Guidance*, op. cit., p. 56 paragraph 7.15 (refers to the RPG 3 Nov. 1991).

6   *The Lavender Hill Mob*, (UK: Ealing, 1951), director: Charles Crichton.

7   Discussed in Chapter 1.

8   *L.A.Story* (USA: Guild/Rastar, 1991), director: Mick Jackson.

9   *La Dolce Vita* (Italy/France: 1959), director: Federico Fellini. This is an insight of Paul Davies.

10   The demand to 'sing doo wah diddy' actually occurs at the film's denouement.

11   Jean-Paul Sartre, quoted in Mary Douglas, *Purity and Danger: An Analysis of the Concepts of Pollution and Taboo*, (London: Routledge & Kegan Paul, 1966), p. 38. See discussion in Chapter 4.

12   P.L. Travers, *Mary Poppins in the Park*, (London: Peter Davies, 1962).

13   *The Chain* (UK: Quintet/County Bank/Channel 4 (Victor Glynn), 1984), director: Jack Gold.

14   Doris Lessing, *The Four Gated City*, (UK: Granada Publishing, 1972).

15   Ibid., p. 33.

16   S.E. Rasmussen, *London, The Unique City*, (USA/UK: MIT Press, 1982), p. 28.

17   The so-called Poll-Tax Riots.

18   Lessing, op. cit., p. 27.

19   Ibid.

20   *Four in the Morning* (UK: West One, 1965), director: Anthony Simmons.

21   *Frenzy* (UK: Universal/Alfred Hitchcock, 1972), director: Alfred Hitchcock.

22   *On Westminster Bridge* by William Wordsworth; *Waterloo Sunset*, by Ray Davies (a song by the Kinks).

23   Government Office for London, *Strategic Planning Guidance for the River Thames*, (London: HMSO, 1997).

24   The comments of the architect Piers Gough were characteristic: 'For Piers Gough, on top form, the Thames "represents a wild space", and is "not a river to mess around on."

He heaped scorn on the idea that one could simply do "a study" on the Thames as if that could embrace each riparian borough's peculiar relationship with the river. "It's rather like going to Brighton and saying the sea goes all the way to America."' David Taylor, Summary of 'The Potential of the Thames: "A New Heart For London" 14.2.96', the *Architects' Journal*, 22 February 1996, p. 17.

25    *Our Mutual Friend*, Charles Dickens, 1868 edition.

26    'Bitzer', said Thomas Gradgrind. 'Your definition of a horse.'

'Quadruped. Graminivorous. Forty teeth, namely, twenty-four grinders, four eye-teeth, and twelve incisive. Sheds coat in the spring; in marshy countries, sheds coat in the spring; in marshy countries sheds hoofs, too. Hoofs hard, but requiring to be shod with iron. Age known by marks in mouth.' This (and much more) Bitzer.

'Now girl number twenty', said Mr. Gradgrind. 'You know what a horse is.' *Hard Times*, Charles Dickens, (1854) Book the First. Sowing, Chapter 2.

27    Dickens, *Our Mutual Friend*, op. cit., Book the First. The Cup and the Lip. Chapter XI, 'Podsnappery'.

28    Dickens, *Our Mutual Friend*, op. cit., Book the First. The Cup and the Lip. Chapter I, 'On the Look-Out'.

29    Dickens, *Our Mutual Friend*, op. cit., Book the First. The Cup and the Lip. Chapter III, 'Another Man'.

# Endpiece

The Endpiece traces the strands – often invisible – of some theoretical assumptions that run through three elements of the book. The first is that apparently *natural* or objective characteristics of space can be interpreted in terms of capitalist activity, particularly the pursuit of profit. The second is that the quest for *purity*, expressed by taboos against pollution, permeates architectural and urban practice. And the third is that fictions, particularly in film and the novel, can be used in a number of ways to reveal unseen workings of architecture. In *Walls Have Feelings*, I have set out both to make connections across a range of scales, from the architectural detail and the interior, to city strategy; and, in apparent contradiction, to encourage ways of thinking about space that transgress the book's own categories. An underlying paradox of the book is that imposition of structure may be necessary to comprehend and undertake such liberating and creative transgression.

This text uses the privileges of fiction. It shifts between one technique for deciphering space and another. At times one or the other, or both, disappear from view. And at other times all three approaches are brought into play. In teaching modern architectural history, the work from which the book springs, I have had recourse to all of these approaches. In the Endpiece, I try to indicate what the interconnections and disjunctures between the three views could be. To begin, however, I first want to outline the relevance of each approach one by one.

## Capitalism

### The Division of Labour

The operations of the division of labour, that is, the tendency of capitalism to divide production into a growing number of separated tasks, cannot be understood without recognition of another fundamental *spatial* division, which is also necessary to the capitalist system. That is the division between the place of work and the place of residence.[1] The division between home and work

> means that the struggle of labour to control the social conditions of its own existence
> splits into two seemingly independent struggles. The first, located in the workplace, is

over the wage rate, which provides the purchasing power for consumption goods, and the conditions of work. The second, fought in the place of residence, is against secondary forms of exploitation and appropriation represented by merchant capital, landed property and the like.[2]

The division of labour has a major impact not only on the material production of space, but on the scientific and technical understandings of space. These understandings are needed by the state in order to impose its own spatial will.[3]

> It was no accident, therefore, that the tightening of the monetary, spatial, and chronological nets in the latter half of the nineteenth century was accompanied by the rise of distinctive professions each with its own corner on the knowledge required to give coherence to those nets . . . the power of engineers and managers, economists and architects, systems analysts and experts in industrial organisation, could not be taken lightly. It became powerfully embedded in key state and corporate functions as planning became the order of the day. Intellectual conflicts over the meanings of money, space, and time had and continue to have very real material effects. The conflict over modernity and design in architecture, for example, is more than a conflict over taste and aesthetics. It deals directly with the question of the proper framing of the urban process in space and time.[4]

## Ideology

More particular to contemporary Marxism is the assumption in the book which is influenced by both Henri Lefebvre and David Harvey. Architecture, its constructions and urban strategies, are made acceptable to society via a set of ideas and assumptions which *conceal* the fact that architecture is an economic product, and subject above all to economic interests, i.e. making a profit. So the division of labour carries with it

> a dissolving and disintegrating ideology that meets the requirements of the market and the social division of labour by promoting fragmented intellectual skills.[5]

The architectural impact of this notion is summarised by Walter Benjamin in his description of the rift between home and work in mid-19th-century Paris, discussed in Chapter 4:

> For the private citizen, for the first time the living-space became distinguished from the place of work. The former constituted itself as the interior. The office was its

complement. The private citizen who in the office took reality into account required of the interior that it should support him in his illusions.[6]

Chapter 4 discusses how the interior takes on an actively ideological role. It supports illusions that in their turn keep the wheels of profit-making oiled. So the interior works as a kind of spatial compensation for clearly experienced exploitation at work. Because the mechanisms of economic exploitation are more obvious at work, this direct ideological-concealing role of the interior is only possible once the two places – work and home – have been divided in space.

Spatial constructions may act ideologically, in the specifically Marxist sense that they represent ideas and ideals that both serve the interest of the economic class in power, and conceal the workings of that interest. This does not mean their form is under current ideological *control*. The imposed boundaries of the past may come back to haunt the present. So Harvey writes that:

> The urban process . . . appears as both fundamental to the perpetuation of capitalism and a primary expression of its inner contradictions now expressed as produced external constraints. Capitalism has to confront the consequences of its urban structurations at each moment in its history. The reduced second natures become the raw materials out of which new configurations of capitalist activity . . . must be wrought.[7]

The version of Marxism assumed here is dialectical. What I mean by that is a volatile and active interchange between ideas, the structures that represent those ideas (art as much as the legal system) and the economic climate that prevails. I use here notions of both pollution and fiction in varying relationship to the economic shapers of urban architecture.

## Purity and Pollution Taboos

The horror film *The Fly* was first made in 1958 and then remade in 1986.[8] In both versions the theme is the same: a scientist called Brundle attempts to develop a new form of transportation that entails dematerialising the body into atoms, and reassembling it in another place, using a device called a 'teleport'. The experiment goes fine until a fly enters the teleport by mistake. As a consequence, the genes of the scientist and the fly get muddled up and he becomes a hybrid – Brundlefly. The defined and delineated classes of man and fly are thereby transgressed and the result is successfully revolting. In the later version of the film, to make matters worse, the scientist has sex with a reporter, who subsequently dreams that she has given birth to a grub.

The anthropologist Mary Douglas, in trying to identify the genesis of pollution taboos, states that 'dirt is matter out of place'.[9] What is so vividly repulsive is not the grub itself, but the fact that it is present in the body of a woman – that is, *out of place*. This taboo is against transgression between established classes: it is Douglas's explanation of Jewish dietary law as defined in the Old Testament book of Leviticus. She rejects the normal common-sense explanation of these taboos, which tells us, for example, that shellfish are forbidden because they are more liable to deterioration than fish. Instead, the argument she uses to explain Leviticus' list of rules is that animals whose characteristics straddle two *classes* – such as those that both swim and walk on land, like crabs – are the ones condemned as abominable, dirty and hybrid:

> These shall ye eat that are in the waters: whatsoever hath fins and scales in the waters, in the seas, and in the rivers them shall ye eat. And all that have not fins and scales in the seas, and in the rivers, of all that move in the waters . . . they shall be an abomination unto . . . All fowls that creep, going upon all four, shall be an abomination unto you.[10]

Under Douglas's thesis, matter is classified in terms of identifiable and clearly delineated *form*, in order to establish what is polluted and taboo. 'Pollution dangers strike when form has been attacked.'[11] *Social well-being (purity) is identified quite literally in the form or the edge of form defined in opposition to a 'sea of formlessness'.*[12] The sea of formlessness is made of everything unclassifiable, against which form must defend itself. As indicated in Chapter 1, Douglas goes on to distinguish four kinds of social pollution, which vary according to the vulnerability of the defining edge (the line which delineates the pure form under threat):

> the first is danger pressing on external boundaries; the second, danger from transgressing the internal lines of a system; the third, danger in the margins of the lines . . . [and] danger from internal contradiction, when some of the basic postulates are denied by other basic postulates, so that at certain points the system seems to be at war with itself.[13]

To extrapolate from Douglas's explanation, Leviticus' forbidden creatures have in common with Brundlefly the characteristics which make them dirty and abominable. They straddle two classes; their edges are unclear and difficult to delineate; they do not have identifiable form which can be categorised; and they cannot be reduced to an original set of parts or classes.

From these principles, we can, paradoxically, arrive at a number of categories ourselves which allow us to class the formal consequences of pollution taboos.

## Smearing

As Douglas herself vividly makes clear in her quotation of Jean-Paul Sartre's essay on viscosity,[14] the transgressor has identifiably formal characteristics. The line is crucial in delineating a clear edge against trespass. It follows that the viscous, things which do not of themselves respect edges, and which are difficult to put a line around, is to be resisted.

> The viscous is a state half-way between solid and liquid. It is like a cross-section in a process of change. It is unstable, but it does not flow. It is soft, yielding and compressible . . . it attacks the boundary between myself and it.[15]

## Classification and Ordering

The Leviticus example demonstrates that classification is all-important. To systematise things in this way, we need clearly identifiable characteristics. As we have seen, characteristics which straddle two classes will define the object as polluted and dirty. In buildings, architecture and the city we would expect to see a virtue made of the delineation of *border*. Following from this, our own ordering system might include:

### Rationality

This way of ordering the world using sets of identifiable characteristics is considered rational. We appeal to reason in order to convince ourselves and others that we are correct in our terms of classification. The guarantee of rationality is in turn associated with capability of the object which we want to classify to be reduced to a set of original parts.

### Original parts or elements

The original parts that we can, so to speak, boil things down into are, by virtue of the fact that they cannot be further reduced, pure and clean. Great store is set by the authentic. If you are uncertain of something's parentage, you can be sure it is a bastard.

### Specialisation

If there is unarguable virtue attached to the reduction of an object into parts, it follows that specialisation – whether in ideas or objects – is a good thing.

### Classicism

Classicism is therefore understood as a style which imposes purity of part, category and order, via a set of rules which depend on the imposition of absolute border, in the form of the firm delineation of architectural elements.

## The decorative

The decorative is that which undermines or challenges the firmness of category and delineating border. It has fuzzy edges, and renders the clear impure and muddy.

Even without the benefit of these extrapolations on the theme that 'dirt is matter out of place', the idea of a struggle against dirt itself moves unusually easily across established genres, intellectual disciplines and spheres of interest, and lends itself to the transgression between common metaphor and material description. Who, for example, is really sure whether the expression *ethnic cleansing* is literal or figurative? The *metaphor* of dirt in the city was a spur to the great 19th- and 20th-century movements of city reform. Again, it was at one and the same time a crusading metaphor, and literally true: dirt and pollution caused untold disease. Indeed, Jonathan Raban has written that the *idea* of dirt 'subsumes the sheer imaginative cumbersomeness of the city which makes us . . . incapable of distinguishing its parts from its whole',[16] and that in relation to England, 'the single feature of the city which has adhered most strongly to writers' minds is its dirt, and dirt is one of the few objects whose moral connotation is as definite and public as its physical characteristics'.[17] Dirt, then, significantly subsumes the *categories and orders* of the city, by being in some over-riding way true. François Maspero describes how in 1935 Aubervilliers in the Parisian suburbs was a 'chemical town' and 'land of death', 'a concentration of "dirty industries" considered undesirable inside the walls of Paris'.[18] And Louis Chevalier has shown how an area of the city which is designated an anomaly (i.e. which does not readily fit in one category or another), and unfitting to the desired urban order, not only is designated dirty, but literally begins to acquire dirt and collect things-out-of-place – the material symptoms of the thing we call urban neglect.

> Beyond the specific filthiness of les Halles there was the filth of Paris, of which les Halles was the recipient . . . their neighbourhood was the dump where Parisians threw everything they no longer wanted . . . One found the strangest things, transported from who knows what part of Paris, thrown in the streets around the markets.[19]

In the face of this transgressive dirt, the over-arching activity of architecture and building construction can be described as the assertion of order.

## Fiction

Since Sigmund Freud's *The Interpretation of Dreams*, the status of interpretation itself has changed. The importance of the dream becomes *precisely what you remember*, nothing more. The elusive whole which memory itself imagines it can retrieve becomes secondary, a mythic, almost ancestral realm. And so interpretation, the text, is the primary site of enquiry.

What happens if we accept that architecture does tangibly exist, not as a pristine, impervious whole, but in the perception of the beholder? If fictional representations of the architecture and the city are understood as the architectural equivalent of the dream record, then their entire status can change. This does not mean that literary codes are directly applied to spaces – because, as Lefebvre says, this would reduce the space 'to the status of a *message* and the inhabiting of it to the status of a *reading*'.[20] But, currently, fictions are accepted at best as interesting, but subordinate, parallel commentaries to mainstream architectural history. This official history uses the vocabulary of specialist knowledge – formal, constructional and so on – to present the profession's assertions in irreproachable terms. By contrast, the modern fictional voice starts from the admission that its narrative is personal and one among many.

The following analytical possibilities exist in using fiction to decipher space.

## Allegory

Christine Buci-Glucksmann discusses Walter Benjamin's own interest in the fictional form of allegory. What is important is the possibility that 'reality exists independently of the languages by which it is made available so that its real nature remains ineffable and hidden. This hidden quality of reality can only be . . . expressed by symbol, by allegory or parable.'[21] Chapter 2 looks at two allegorical fictions, created as installations with the intent to penetrate through the received wisdom of the technical.

## Narrative

The *story* of how a space is used, as an adjunct to character and action, reveals an unspoken history of the role of space within the city. Space can be a character acting independently within the narrative itself. Chapter 5 discusses how the play on 'Her' in the title of Jean-Luc Godard's film *Two or Three Things I Know About Her*, (1967), to refer directly both to the city of Paris and to the many-headed prostitute subject, makes this deliberately clear.[22]

## Structural Pattern

The experience of living in the modern city is so disjunctive that the habitual deciphering of everyday life, which we all do, can be described as the fictional imagination's attempt to describe a pattern.

> To live in a city is to live in a community of people who are strangers to each other. You have to act on hints and fancies for they are all that the mobile and cellular nature of city life will allow you. You expose yourself in, and are exposed to by others, fragments,

> isolated signals, bare disconnected gestures, jungle cries and whispers that resist all your attempts to unravel their meaning, their consistency.[23]

This is such a common, consciously recognised experience, that the fictional structuring of the city through pattern is a characteristic of most of the great novels of the 19th and 20th centuries. Unlike the smaller scales of architecture and construction, fiction is acceptable as a form of structuring the large-scale *experience* of the city in even the most technical of publications.[24]

There is a related paradox of the both/and variety which defines the fictional voice, and it is again inherent in the notion of transgression. Simultaneously with the single fictional voice's implicit multiplicity, for the duration of the narrative, it has absolute authority. In other words, you have to run with it. For the post-structuralist this fictional operation is doubly paradoxical, as it re-introduces the pleasures of structuralism's all-seeing eye. The use of fiction within architectural theory assumes that the reader can, as when watching a film, voluntarily suspend their own disbelief. Thus, far-reaching structural connections can be understood at one and the same time as fictional, and, for the duration of the argument, be accepted as absolutely true. The implication is that fiction has a peculiarly transgressive role in challenging the primacy of the specialist. The combination of the two structuralist approaches in this book, pollution taboo and Marxism, might *explain* the rise of the specialist, but it takes the active operation of fiction to *subvert* her/his authority. The transgressive role of fiction means both that, like feminism, it legitimates architectural and urban insights and experiences of the non-expert (as manifest in films and novels), and that specialist knowledge itself is subjected to a wider structure than its own self-validating technical terms. This allows fictional insight to be considered on the same terms as the insights of the non-expert.

A number of cross-overs between these three deciphering methods – capitalism, pollution taboo, fiction – can operate.

## A Modified Structuralism

The notion of a *fiction* modifies the universality and truth implied in both the idea of pollution taboo, and in the notion that human affairs are ultimately driven by economics. It means that these two ways of structuring events can, themselves, be thoroughly exploited, but at the same time be treated as fictions, as texts themselves 'up for' interpretation.[25] You can 'try' big ideas out, as you might try a novel or a film. This is useful, because the drawback to rejecting structuralism's claims to objective truth is that it has left us with the impression that statements we make about architecture and the city can be, at best, only ever partial or fragmentary. Attempts to get at an overall theory that 'explains' things are out of favour; there is a fashion for the flash of insight, the little observation. The possibility of furthering under-standing by making bold connections between apparently disparate circumstances is denied. One consequence for the city is that, in default of an over-riding theory, once again decisions get given over to the specialist, and problems are confirmed as subject to technical expertise rather than to general knowledge.

So my argument is that an intentionally paradoxical way of looking at the world can thread through explorations of architecture and the city. Structural connections are confidently assumed, but they may be treated on a par with a kind of fictional coincidence: they sustain the story, and allow us to follow the argument.[26] But how can you assert the primacy of structure and at the same time examine the potential of moments where it is deliberately challenged? This dilemma, it seems to me, is familiar to Marxists. Lefebvre, writing immediately following the massive transgression of spatial, social and political structures of the May 1968 events in France,[27] states this paradox:

> a serious concern with spontaneity implies at the same time a delineation of spontaneity. This must be done in the name of a theory which pure spontaneity tends to ignore.[28]

Elsewhere, he cautions against the static nature of structuralism, citing Herbert Marcuse on linguistics. He points to 'linguistics' . . . particularly dangerous role. Operating in the reified world of discourse, it purges thought and speech of *contradictions and transgressions*'[29] [emphasis added]. The play of action in the world – here with transgressive and challenging implications – and its analysis as a set of structural connections can be thought of as a kind of mini version of the dialectic. It is a two-way interaction between economic forces and the superstructures of society – art, politics, ideas – which drives progress on a macro scale.

## Form and Theoretical and Physical Structures

But this interaction, between structure itself and challenges to its own categories and edges, is not just a theoretical theme in this book. It can also be understood in concrete architectural form. In the churches of the Baroque architect Bernardo Vittone, there is a relationship between their physical, delineated structure, and the spatial and material methods he uses to challenge and transgress the viewers' rational expectations of that structure. This is apparent in his development of the double-skinned vault. At his chapel at Vallinotto in Piedmont, Italy, Vittone constructs a structural inner skeleton which holds a dome, and which also works as a windowed canopy onto a series of outer vaults depicting pictures of heaven (Fig. 1).

The inner skeleton is an entirely visible comprehensible structure, whereas the structure of the outer vaults is entirely hidden. The inner skeleton acts effectively as

**Endpiece 1** Interior view, chapel at Vallinotto, Piedmont, Italy (1739): Bernardo Vittone.

**Endpiece 2** Section drawing, chapel at Vallinotto, Piedmont, Italy (1739): Bernardo Vittone.

a structure understandable through reason, through which the worshipper views heaven floating above them. In a nifty reversal of expectations, it is the *illusion* of heaven which is illuminated with the *real* light of earth, via a hidden window, while the tangible, earth-bound, inner structure remains dark. It is through the clear delineation of this inner containing structure that, again paradoxically, the illusion of heaven above us is made apparently *more real*. In this work by Vittone there is literally a base structure – the inner skeleton – and a super-structure – the outer vaults. The one is literally down-to-earth, while the other depicts possibilities beyond the earthly, beyond the immediate material reality of the inner vault. The possibilities of the one cannot be 'read' without the other – they work dialectically. To achieve this, the purity of delineated architectural categories, its clearly defined visible elements of dome, column, wall and window, are deliberately transgressed. The section shows that you cannot see where domes are supported by columns, where columns meet the earth, or where a window begins or ends (Fig. 2).

It is particularly in the field of *formal*, physical identification of transgression, that Douglas's definitions of pollution taboos are fruitful. Any designer or builder experiences the decisions they make on an immediate, material level. However restricted, choices do exist a surprising number of times in the working day, concerning this, rather than that, shape, component or material. What I offer to the reader in this book is a way of interrogating the specific details of architectural and urban *form* illuminated by *non-formal* issues – cultural, economic and political. Architecture is a practical subject massively loaded with meaning for culture at large: everyone other than those, like surveyors, in whose professional interests it is to ignore such uncomfortable complexity, acknowledges this as a matter of course. My intention is to bring the two aspects, the practical specifics and cultural meaning, to bear on each other. This is very difficult; making simply passing references to the cultural in formal analysis, and vice versa, is much easier. To read David Harvey's examination of the Sacré Cœur in Paris[30] is a real disappointment because it does not deal with the specific spatial or material qualities of that place; to read architectural theorist Colin Rowe's detailed examination of the formal properties of Le Corbusier's entry for the Palace of the Soviet's competition,[31] a piece which ignores the entire political context of this clearly loaded project, is equally frustrating.

One of the reasons why the work of the Marxist Benjamin is so important is that he is able to focus down on an identifiable figure through which to muse on the workings, veils and manifestations of capitalist interests. With characteristic compression he says:

> Ambiguity is the *figurative* appearance of the dialectic, the law of dialectic at a standstill. [emphasis added] This standstill is Utopia, and the dialectical image therefore a dream image. The commodity clearly provides such an image: as fetish. The arcades, which are both house and stars, provide such an image. And such an image is provided by the whore, who is seller and commodity in one.[32]

Benjamin's work on the arcades points the way: its space is not *just* a product, for it is also a fetish. It seeks to cover something else up; it is ideological. Benjamin implies that the arcades' very *ambiguity* – both 'house and stars' – is the reason why this particular architectural commodity is especially fruitful ground for unravelling the capitalist dialectic.

In this context, the films *Alfie*[33] and *Darling*[34] provide material in Chapter 4 for examining the architectural minutiae of the 1960s' office interior: the sideboard and the padded wall. In it I discuss the schism Benjamin speaks of between home and work, which is at the outset gendered. Woman is established in the home, the man at work; the association of the woman with the interior, the fixed decorative, is set up. This division is dependent on physical changes to the city: in Paris the Haussmann road projects, in London the suburban railway system – the fate of the interior is inextricably bound up with, first, the world outside it, and second, with the situation of women in time and space. Once post-war economics dictate that women *en masse* go to work in the office, the character of the interior changes. New system-building erases the decorative interior in the home: it becomes depicted as merely the other side of the wall. Effectively it becomes part of the urban scene, the world outside: a place where the flaneur Alfie can move in and out at will, sampling different women.

In the context of women at work, the decorative attaches itself to women themselves: the painted dolly bird pictured against stark walls becomes a kind of peripatetic interior. At the site of utter exclusion of female power, the executive suite and boardroom, the decorative again breaks free from the surface of the woman's body and into the interior beyond. While the home and working office beyond become an efficient machine, the boardroom becomes feminised: a romanticised version of the home, dependent as all romanticism on a sense of loss. Grained timber panelling abounds; walls are soft and padded; the subversively anti-modernist hidden storage space makes a surreptitious come-back. One object in the boardroom interior becomes purely fetishistic in Benjamin's sense of the word: the sideboard or credenza.

In *Sabrina Fair*,[35] this fetish is a remnant from an idealised kitchen: a feminine magic carpet object that can magically span the rift between office and home. Audrey Hepburn, visiting the successful but unfulfilled executive Humphrey Bogart in his executive suite, puts on an apron and magically conjures up a wholesome meal from its unpromising urban cocktail contents. The boardroom, site of the harshest economic decisions, veils itself as the place where all is right with the world: the rift between home and work, the universal characteristic of developed capitalism, is healed.

### Fiction, Meaning and Architecture

The importance of fiction, and in particular film, is that its own intent to tell a story – even in the widest possible sense – means that its use of architecture is inevitably self-consciously loaded with meaning. I am struck by the way a film-maker will commonly spend much longer determining how the artefacts of architects, and other urban designers, are to be filmed, than was originally spent designing the artefacts themselves in the first place. In Roman Polanski's films *Repulsion*[36] and *Rosemary's Baby*,[37] explored in Chapter 3, the role of the detail is crucial both to the entire action of the film, and to the viewer's saturation in the fictional meaning the producer is trying to convey. In these two films, the litany of illegitimate piercings of the skins of the heroine's respective apartments acts both as a metaphor for the violation of the female body, and as crucial incidents in forwarding the narrative. In *Repulsion*, the camera traces the onslaught of a minute series of cracks in the plasterwork of Catherine Deneuve's apartment. At the film's climax, the walls begin literally to smear the edge between Deneuve and themselves. In *Rosemary's Baby*, the corridor is worryingly ambiguous: neither in Rosemary's flat nor in the neighbouring flat, a hidden door allows a devastating penetration of Rosemary herself and her apartment by the devil worshippers next door. In each film the indeterminate, impure edge has nightmarish consequences.

It is not just the film-maker who encapsulates this sophisticated architectural sensibility. Importantly, the viewer's comprehension of architectural clues is assumed, and by the evident success of the films I have used as examples in this book, we can conclude that the assumption is right.

## Form and Politics

So the notion of transgression subsumes both the formal and the political. But what kind of relationship really exists? Is it conceivable that a complete correspondence could occur between a visual logic carried to the extreme in built architecture, and a 'logic of society' – the strategies inspired by a state bureaucracy?[38]

The purport of Douglas's *Purity and Danger* is that the political – the assertion of power in a particular society – has a formal expression in the excluding characteristics of pollution taboos. Douglas points out that:

> Pollution dangers strike when form has been attacked. Thus we would have a triad of powers controlling fortune and misfortune: first, formal powers wielded by persons representing the formal structure and exercised on behalf of the formal structure; second, formless powers wielded by interstitial persons; third, powers not wielded by any person, but inhering in the structure, which strike against any infraction of form.[39]

What does this mean for architecture? If we observe a concerted re-assertion of clear rules, both of a structure *within* a design, and a structure to apply *to* that design, we should ask two things. One, where is the attack on form against which the architectural rules are reacting? And two, where is the formal structure that is being defended? 'Formal structure' here has the meaning of a societal structure, whose interests are defended by those who shout most loudly for a recall to order.[40]

So, in Chapter 1, the Brutalist hegemony in post-war British architecture is interpreted in the following way. Form was perceived as under attack by a decorative free style associated with the buildings and designs of the 1951 Festival of Britain.[41]

This coincided with an economic need to industrialise the building industry, leading both to the standardisation and to the specialisation of components – in Douglas's terms, the purification of form.[42] Politically, the onset of the Cold War led to (a) a literal re-assertion of physical boundary at the macro-scale – the Iron Curtain, the Berlin Wall – and (b) a need to distance all cultural communities, including the architectural, from the politics and aesthetics of Socialist Realism and instead to project honesty and transparency.[43] On a broader cultural level, the taste for the uncompromising, brutally honest warts-and-all approach was personified in the figure of the Angry Young Man and the Technicolor-rejecting, slice-of-life films of the British New Wave. So in architecture, the formal structure being defended was the purity of pre-war Modernism. The terms of exclusion inherent in Brutalism – against colour, decoration, uncertainty of line, hybrid materials – re-asserted architectural rules in the face of the Anything Goes, picturesque aesthetic of the immediate post-war decade.

At the scale of Marxist spatial analysis of the city and landscape, the formal co-incidence of political and 'pure' interests directly connects the development of capitalism to burgeoning specialisation and fixed delineation. This applies both to space, and to the professional and technical tasks associated with the control of space such as architectural design. The drawing of *immovable lines* around fixed edges was a necessary prerequisite

> for the development of unambiguous definition of property rights in land. Space thus came to be represented, like time and value, *as abstract, objective, homogenous, and universal in its qualities.*[44] [emphasis added]

The regular delineation of space – whether at the micro-scale of a component, as in the post-war building industry, discussed in Chapter 2, or at the macro-scale of the city through zoning, discussed in Chapter 6 – smooths the way to the commodification of space allowing it to be bought or sold as other products.

> Builders, engineers, and architects for their part showed how abstract representations of objective space could be combined with exploration of the concrete malleable properties of materials in space.[45]

For Harvey, the general consolidation of space as universal is ultimately driven not by the tendency towards classification and delineation, but by the forces of capitalism's own expanding tendency to commodify everything.[46]

Once this universal parcelling out of defined space is established, a number of formal consequences accompany it. These work in parallel both with space's delineation, and with its categorisation, attendant on the growing division of labour. Ambiguity of function is cast out. In a powerful and dense passage quoted at the beginning of Chapter 6, Lefebvre describes the social and professional manifestations of what he calls spatial abstraction – the result of this quasi-universal containment of space – coupled with space's atomisation into functions:

> Euclidean space . . . is literally flattened out, confined to a surface . . . The person who sees and knows only how to see, the person who draws and knows only how to put marks on a sheet of paper, the person who drives around and knows only how to drive a car – all contribute in their way to the mutilation of a space which is everywhere sliced up . . . the driver is concerned only with steering himself to his destination and in looking about sees only what he needs to see for that purpose; he thus perceives only his route, which has been materialised, mechanised and technicised and he sees it from one angle only – that of its functionality: speed, readability, facility . . . The reading of space that has been manufactured with readability in mind amounts to a sort of pleonasm, that of *a 'pure' and illusory transparency.* [emphasis added] Space is defined in this context in terms of the perception of an *abstract subject*, such as the driver of a motor vehicle, equipped with a collective common sense, namely the capacity to read the symbols of the highway code, and with a sole organ – the eye – placed in the service of his movement within the visual field. Thus space appears solely in its reduced forms. Volume leaves the field to surface and any overall view surrenders to visual signals spaced out along fixed trajectories already laid down in the 'plan'. An extraordinary – indeed unthinkable, impossible – confusion gradually arises between space and surface, with the latter determining a spatial abstraction which it endows with a half-imaginary, half-real physical existence. This abstract space eventually becomes the simulacrum of a full space . . . Travelling – walking or strolling about – becomes an actually experienced, gestural simulation of the formerly urban activity of encounter, of movement amongst concrete existences.[47]

In opposition to this tendency, during the events of May 1968 in the Paris region, self-consciously transgressive political activities burgeoned. In particular, the established intellectual categories were rejected, in part by virtue of their uncritical mirroring of the economic divisions of labour.[48] This then impacted to explode the spatial abstraction of the city.

> During those days the dichotomies between activity and passivity, between private life and social life, between the demands of daily life and those of political life, between leisure and work and the places associated with them, between spoken and written language, between action and knowledge, all these dichotomies disappeared in the *streets,*

*amphitheatres and factories* [emphasis added] . . . Horrified and impotent, the adherents of norms witness the sequence of transgressions. They are unable to conceive of the initial transgression: the crossing of the border that 'normally' separates the political and non-political areas, and the ensuing emancipation.[49]

Like the division of labour itself, these acts had their formal spatial expression. Chapter 5 describes how key catalyst of the May events was the demand at Nanterre for 'libre circulation'. Nanterre, where Lefebvre taught, is a post-war Parisian suburb, a university by the motorway made of anonymous concrete blocks. Danny Cohn-Bendhit, like a latter-day Alfie, led the protests in favour of free circulation. What was being demanded was the right to freely circulate in and out of the bedrooms of female students: the transgression of literal, physical boundaries in the name of freedom.

## Structural Truth

The imperative to make architecture 'structurally true' pioneered by Ruskin, Pugin and others in the 19th century, manifests all the characteristics of a pollution taboo played out. Fundamentally important is the idea that such truth must be *seen*. To avoid any fuzziness or bastardisation or transgression at the junction between two parts, architecture must visibly reveal how it stands up, and what element supports what. This means that the distinction between parts must be as clearly drawn as possible to avoid any accusation of obfuscation or tinkering with the truth. Despite its association with morality and Socialism, structural truth works as a successful partner in the promotion by the building industry of differentiated constructional roles, and hence increasing specialisation. To pass the truth test, one specialist component must not only be guaranteed absolutely distinguishable from another; it must not trespass on the other's specialist role.

Chapter 1 looks at how the British Brutalist movement connected the apparently unrefined qualities of materials, used in their original, irreducible condition, with an attempt to 'face up' to the realities of the conditions of post-war life, and 'drag a rough poetry',[50] in Peter Smithson's words, out of these conditions of the everyday. The assumption is that covering up brute reality, whether social or cultural, is equivalent in the realm of building construction to covering up pure, undefiled materials and elements. Hence the act of revealing, still at a *constructional* level, acquires for architects a moral authority at a *cultural* level. For the philosopher Theodor Adorno, writing in *The Jargon of Authenticity*, 'the more earnestly the jargon sanctifies its everyday world . . . the more sadly does the jargon mix up the literal with the figurative'.[51] This mix-up between the literal and figurative, observed in relation to the idea of dirt, emerges in the related field of structural truth. As Lefebvre observes:

The oddness of this space . . . is that it is at once homogeneous and compartmentalised. It is also simultaneously limpid and deceptive; in short fraudulent. Falsely true – 'sincere', so to speak; not the object of a false consciousness, but rather the locus and medium of the generation (or production) of false consciousness.[52]

## Rationality and Irrationality

Another 'take' on the tension between structure and transgression concerns ideas of rationality and irrationality. This related pair of dualities, is, at first sight, less a formal issue and more to do with the self-conscious expression of ideas. Yet there are moments in the rhetoric of architectural production when reason is overtly appealed to. Architects working in the 18th century could hardly escape the pervasiveness of *soit disant* rationality, while our own contemporary building component industry is wedded to the accepted formal demonstrations of rationality – numbering systems, specialisations, categories within categories. Architects have to regularise their activities and submit themselves to accepted rationalities in the fields which affect them, in particular legal and financial ones. In the broader spatial terms which affect city scale, Lefebvre observes that:

A classical (Cartesian) rationality thus appears to underpin various spatial distinctions and divisions. Zoning . . . which is responsible – precisely – for fragmentation, break-up and separation under the umbrella of a bureaucratically decreed unity, *is conflated with the rational capacity to discriminate.* [emphasis added] The assignment of functions . . . 'on the ground', becomes indistinguishable from the kind of analytical activity that discerns differences. What is being covered up here is a moral and political order: the specific power that organises these conditions, with its specific socio-economic allegiance, seems to flow directly from the Logos – that is from a 'consensual' embrace of the rational. Classical reason has apparently undergone a convulsive degeneration into technological and technocratic rationality; *this is the moment of its transformation into its opposite – into the absurdity of a pulverised reality.* [emphasis added] It is on the ground too that the state-bureaucratic order . . . simultaneously achieves self-actualisation and self-concealment, fuzzying its image in the crystal clear air of functional and structural readability.[53]

The 'Her' of Godard's *Two or Three Things I Know About Her*, investigated in Chapter 5, addresses both the various prostitute protagonists and the city of Paris herself. While in the Polanski films the violation of the heroine's bodily surface and the surface of her apartment interior works in synchronicity, in the Godard film the parallel analogy refers to the rupture at urban scale. So 'the absurdity of a pulverised reality' is, specifically, the building in the 1960s of the giant *Périphérique* ring-road around Paris: a constructional project which renders, in terms of technological rationality, the previous spatial connections of the city nonsensical. In the face of the onslaught of bulldozers, the prostitute, draped in the colours of the Tricolour, tells us that she dreams 'she has been torn into a thousand pieces'. Like a visual illustration of Lefebvre's spatial abstraction, Godard's depiction of the new city of Paris is an architect's model of orthogonal blocks, created from the packaging of international commodities.

In opposition to this classical rationality, the closing image of Godard's film is a bunch of flowers thrown over the delineation of the Paris region: edgeless, undelineated and uncategorised.

Of the three theoretical approaches presented here, two (Marxism and the structuralist analysis of pollution taboo) use the apparent paradox of rational systems to unearth the irrational in human activity. Only fiction does not assert that its role is to systematise an otherwise irrational world. Yet the thrust of both Marxism and Douglas's structuralist work is not just to unearth the irrational; what gives it teeth is the way in which it systematically demonstrates the irrational outcomes of apparently quite rational systems. The aim of the Marxist analysis of the apparently rational circulation of capital is to demonstrate the irrational, dysfunctional outcomes of market economics – crises of over-production, world recessions, etc. In a kind of equivalence, Lefebvre suggests above that, with the development of capitalism, classicism undergoes a degeneration which transforms it into a kind of remorseless a-logicality, precisely by the operation *ad absurdum* of its system of logic.

This remorseless a-logicality is to be read at a micro- as well as macro-level. Buildings replete with what Lefebvre calls 'structural readability' can nevertheless become logistically dysfunctional. The architectural rules of purity, legibility and honesty promoted by Brutalism dictate that elements should not be covered up, and that structural function be clearly expressed. Chapter 2 looks at how a 1960s' barracks building in Shorncliffe, Kent, underlines that the concrete 'stub columns' are working structurally to hold the building up. They are sloped back to honestly prove that they sit on the internal skin of its cavity wall, behind the external skin. In the building's eagerness to reveal its structural honesty, the sloping concrete interrupts the continuity of the external skin, it conducts any water around in the direction of the interior – and so potentially compromises what is the accepted constructional role of an outside wall: to keep out water. A system of logic operating *ad absurdum*?

For Douglas, too, it is not sufficient to refer to hygiene as the rational source of pollution taboos: she unearths a complex system of taboos against intrusions which bring no objective harm whatsoever. This is why one can't understand what is going on by simple reference to rationality. As Bryan Turner has said:

> From the point of view of an alternative history of capitalism it is the *irrational* [emphasis added] violence of passions and the destructive energies of human sexuality which are important . . . This perversity of human rationalism is probably best captured by the ambivalent figures of Benjamin's Angel and Baudelaire's prostitute, by the flaneur and the bohemian, rather than the penny-pinching, rationally organised, capitalist entrepreneur.[54]

Turner notes that the arch-chronicler of human rationality, the sociologist Max Weber, argued that

> [the] origins of capitalist rationality lay not in a rational world view, but, on the contrary, in the deeply irrational impulse of salvation within the terrifying theology of Calvin. In short, the roots of modern rationality lay in religious irrationality.[55]

But the totality of religious experience, after all, appeals to both reason (this is inherent both in any moral code and in the patterns of institutional organisation) and, at one and the same time, to the suspension of reason: witness the belief in normally incredible happenings such as the Resurrection and Assumption of Christ. The Baroque is a period of particular interest in this context. Its overt Counter-Reformatory mission can be understood as a conscious intent to bypass reason by appealing, as in St Ignatius Loyola's excercises, to all five senses in order to seduce the errant Protestants back to the true church. The example of Vittone's work cited above, poised between the Enlightenment and the Baroque, serves as an archetypal and masterly simultaneous revelation of reason – the transparent logic of the inner skeletal structure – and divine experience which transgresses reason's earthbound rules – expressed in the structural mystery of Vallinotto's outer shells.

   This subversive quality of the Baroque is not only architectural: Buci-Glucksmann in *Baroque Reason* makes it clear that the idea of *progress* is challenged by the Baroque. She associates the idea of 'progress' in modernity with the 'great classical form', of a fulfilled meaning of history corresponding to reality, of truth as a system and of the subject as identity and centre. Antithetically to this, the Baroque presents from the beginning quite a different, 'post-modern' conception of reality in which the instability of forms in movement opens onto 'the reduplicated and reduplicable structure of all reality: enchanted illusion and disenchanted world'.[56] Progress is inherent in the Marxist analysis of capital, in that inevitable economic crisis will worsen until a properly rational system of production and distribution, i.e. Communism, replaces it. That this rejection of progress is not, however, incompatible with a Marxist outlook is indicated by Buci-Glucksmann's citation of Benjamin's own understanding of the opposition of the two world views, Classicism and the Baroque:

'By its very essence Classicism was not permitted to behold the lack of freedom, the imperfection, the collapse of physical beautiful nature.'[57]

The fiction itself, as an analytical tool, operates as a form of *baroque reason*. It runs counter to the two systematic approaches of Marxism and the structural identification of the operation of pollution taboo. It is without the burden of overt rationality, whether of form or content, and without the need to assert truth or progress.

The proposition of this book as a whole, is that culture at large evidences an untapped spatial and architectural understanding. The site of this understanding is in its fictions. The power of this comprehension is that it itself transgresses imposed categories of specialisation, expertise, professional and political restricted practices. The pity of it is that it remains untapped, both by those very professions and the public who for the most part persist in seeing their own spatial understandings as subject to a 'superior' comprehension. By moving fictional insight to centre stage, it may yet be possible both to kick the technical off its pedestal and reveal its own fictional origins, and to argue for the constructive exploitation of the analysis and insight of the fictions of film and the novel in public discussion of the city's future.

## Notes

1    See Chapter 4.
2    David Harvey, *Consciousness and the Urban Experience*, (Oxford: Blackwell, 1985), p. 38.
3    See Chapter 2.
4    Harvey, op. cit., p. 32.
5    Henri Lefebvre, *The Explosion: Marxism and the French Revolution of May 1968*, (New York: *Monthly Review*, 1969), p. 119.
6    Walter Benjamin, *Charles Baudelaire: A Lyric Poet in the Era of High Capitalism*, (London and New York: Verso, 1983), p. 167.
7    Ibid., p. 273.
8    Kurt Neumann, *The Fly* (USA: Eastman Color Cinemascope TCF, 1958); David Cronenberg, *The Fly* (USA: DeLuxe TCF/Books Film (Stuart Cornfeld), 1986).
9    Mary Douglas, *Purity and Danger: an Analysis of the Concepts of Pollution and Taboo*, (London: Routledge and Kegan Paul, 1966), p. 35.
10   Leviticus 11:9, 10, 20, quoted by Douglas, *Purity and Danger*, p. 41.
11   Douglas, op. cit., p. 104.
12   Ibid., p. 104.

13 Ibid., p. 122.

14 Referred to in Chapters 3 and 6.

15 Douglas, op. cit, p. 38.

16 Jonathan Raban, *Soft City*, (London: Hamish Hamilton, 1974), p. 25.

17 Ibid.

18 François Maspero, *Roissy Express*, (London: Verso, 1992), p. 177.

19 Louis Chevalier, *The Assassination of Paris*, (Chicago: University of Chicago Press, 1994), p. 212.

20 Henri Lefebvre, *The Production of Space*, (Oxford: Blackwell, 1991), p. 7.

21 Turner goes on to say that '[t]his problem is fundamental to the work of Benjamin, whose theory of language has often been neglected in favour of exegesis of his aesthetic theories.' Bryan S. Turner, 'Introduction', Christine Buci-Glucksmann, *Baroque Reason: The Aesthetics of Modernity*, (London: Sage, 1994). Refer to Chapter 2's introductory description of a technical process through analogy.

22 See Chapter 5.

23 Raban, op. cit., p. 7.

24 See, for example, Brendan O'Leary's 'British Farce, French Drama and Tales of Two Cities: Reorganisations of Paris and London Governments 1957–86,' *London Public Administration*, v.65 (Winter 1987), pp. 369–89.

25 Something of this approach informs Buci-Glucksmann's interpretation of Benjamin's own interpretative methodology: 'In the dialectical image the past of a given epoch is always "the past of always". But it presents itself as such only in the eyes of a particular epoch – the one in which humanity, rubbing its eyes, recognises precisely this dream image for what it is. At that moment the historian's task is the interpretation of dreams . . . Faced with the fine totalities of classicism, or with a Marxist Weltanschauung aesthetic, Benjamin therefore emphasises quite a different scanning of history to bring out an archaeology of modernity at its crucial turning points: the seventeenth-century baroque, the nineteenth century of Baudelaire (and not Balzac), the literary avant-garde of the twentieth century.' Buci-Glucksmann, *Baroque Reason*, p. 46.

26 See, for example, in Chapter 6, how each character, artefact and space of Charles Dickens' novel *Our Mutual Friend* links up with the one character of John Harman, who remains invisible except in providing this structural connection in much of the text.

27 Henri Lefebvre taught at the suburban university of Nanterre, where the 'events' were sparked off. The events involved mass demonstrations, student strikes, general strikes and the immobilisation of transport. They were regarded by libertarians and Marxists as a time on the brink of revolution.

28 Lefebvre, *Explosion*, p. 74.

29 Ibid., p. 29.

30    Harvey, *Consciousness and the Urban Experience*, p. 221.

31    Colin Rowe, 'Transparency: Literal and Phenomenal', *The Mathematics of the Ideal Villa and Other Essays*, (Cambridge, Mass.: MIT Press, 1982), p. 160.

32    Benjamin, op. cit., p. 171. See the discussion of the prostitute as urban metaphor in Chapter 5.

33    *Alfie* (UK: Paramount/Sheldrake, 1966), director: Lewis Gilbert.

34    *Darling* (UK: Anglo-Amalgamated/Vic/Appia, 1965), director: John Schlesinger.

35    *Sabrina Fair* (US title *Sabrina*) (USA: Paramount, 1954), director: Billy Wilder.

36    *Repulsion* (UK: Compton/Tekli, 1965), director: Roman Polanski.

37    *Rosemary's Baby* (USA: Paramount/William Castle, 1968), director: Roman Polanski.

38    Lefebvre, *Production of Space*, p. 312. Though admitting such coincidence is improbable, Lefebvre does say that Brasilia seems to be an example.

39    Douglas, op. cit., p. 104; see discussion in Chapter 1.

40    Lionel Esher, *A Broken Wave: The Rebuilding of England 1940–1980*, (London: Allen Lane, 1980), p. 60.

41    Reyner Banham, *The New Brutalism*, (London: The Architectural Press, 1966) pp. 12–13.

42    See Brian Finnimore, *Houses from the Factory: System Building and the Welfare State*, (London: Rivers Oram Press, 1989).

43    Banham, op. cit., p. 13.

44    Harvey, op. cit., p. 13.

45    Ibid.

46    '[A]ll manner of other conceptions of place and space – sacred and profane, symbolic, personal, animistic – could continue to function undisturbed. It took something more to consolidate space, as universal, homogeneous, objective and abstract in most social practices. That "something" was the buying and selling of space as a commodity.' Harvey, op. cit., p. 13.

47    Lefebvre, *Production of Space*, p. 313.

48    This transgression extended to established intellectual categories: 'The movement at first concentrated on specifically economic objectives: buildings, credits, employment, market restraint, imperatives of the division of labour. These old demands – inadequately but forcefully taken over by the bureaucratic trade-union and political apparatus – were soon superseded. The movement began to raise questions of ideology and "values." The question of specialised knowledge came to the fore. This type of knowledge – fragmented, departmentalised – is condemned by the most perceptive students . . . in addition, the students violently attack the form of education, which they accuse of masking the deficiencies of content by high-handedly imposing both ideology and fragmented knowledge.' Lefebvre, *Explosion*, pp. 110–11.

49    Ibid., pp. 115–16.

50  Banham, op. cit., p. 12.

51  Theodor Adorno, *The Jargon of Authenticity*, (London: Routledge & Kegan Paul, 1973), p. 33.

52  Lefebvre, *Production of Space*, pp. 50–1 and 310.

53  Ibid., p. 317.

54  Turner, 'Introduction', Buci-Glucksmann, *Baroque Reason*, p. 34.

55  Ibid., pp. 17–18.

56  Buci-Glucksmann, *Baroque Reason*, p. 134.

57  Walter Benjamin, *The Origin of German Tragic Drama*, (London: New Left Books, 1977), p. 176.

# Bibliography

Roger Absalom, *France: The May Events 1968*, (London: Longman, 1971).

Lyall Addleston, *Building Failures: A Guide to Diagnosis, Remedy and Prevention*, 3rd edition, (London: Architectural Press, 1992).

Theodor Adorno, *The Jargon of Authenticity*, (London: Routledge & Kegan Paul, 1973).

Anthony Aldgate, *Censorship and the Permissive Society – British Cinema and Theatre 1955–1965*, (Oxford: Clarendon Press, 1995).

*Architects' Journal*, 15 November 1967.

*Architects' Journal*, 21 August 1968.

*Architects' Journal*, 4 September 1968.

*Architects' Journal*, 20 November 1968.

*Architects' Journal*, 26 February 1969.

*Architects' Journal*, 23 April 1969.

*Architects' Journal*, 22 February 1996.

*Architectural Design*, April 1957.

*Architectural Record*, May 1968.

Mary Banham and Bevis Hillier, editors, *A Tonic to the Nation: The Festival of Britain 1951*, (London: Thames & Hudson, 1976).

Reyner Banham, *The New Brutalism*, (London: The Architectural Press, 1966).

*Building*, 10 February 1967.

Walter Benjamin, *The Origin of German Tragic Drama*, (London: New Left Books, 1977).

Walter Benjamin, *Charles Baudelaire: A Lyric Poet in the Era of High Capitalism*, (London & New York: Verso, 1983).

Christine Buci-Glucksmann, *Baroque Reason: The Aesthetics of Modernity*, (London: Sage, 1994).

E.J. Carter and Ernö Goldfinger, *The County of London Plan*, (London: Penguin, 1945).

*Chartered Surveyor*, Building Defects Supplement, April 1981.

Louis Chevalier, *The Assassination of Paris*, (Chicago: University of Chicago Press, 1994).

*Concise Oxford Dictionary*, (UK: Oxford University Press, 1963).

Dennis Crompton, 'City Synthesis', The Living City (1963), article reproduced in *A Guide to Archigram 1961–74*, (London: Academy Editions, 1994).

Alan Delgado, *The Enormous File: A Social History of the Office*, (London: John Murray, 1979).

Charles Dickens, *Hard Times*, (1854).

Charles Dickens, *Our Mutual Friend*, (1868).

Mary Douglas, *Purity and Danger: An Analysis of the Concepts of Pollution and Taboo*, (London: Routledge and Kegan Paul, 1966).

Margaret Drabble, editor, *The Oxford Companion to English Literature*, (UK: Oxford University Press, 1998).

Lionel Esher, *A Broken Wave: The Rebuilding of England 1940–1980*, (London: Allen Lane, 1980).

Brian Finnimore, *Houses from the Factory: System Building and the Welfare State*, (London: Rivers Oram Press, 1989).

Adrian Forty, *Objects of Desire: Design and Society 1750–1980*, (London: Thames & Hudson, 1986).

Robert W. Gill, *The Thames and Hudson Manual of Rendering with Pen and Ink*, (London: Thames & Hudson, 1973).

Government Office for London, *Strategic Guidance for London Planning Authorities: Consultation Draft*, (London: HMSO, 1995).

Government Office for London, *Strategic Planning Guidance for the River Thames*, (London: HMSO, 1997).

Greater London Council, *GLC Good Practice Details*, (London: Architectural Press, 1979).

Helen Gurley-Brown, *Sex and the Single Girl*, (USA: NY Pocket, 1963).

Leslie Halliwell (edited by John Walker), *Halliwell's Film Guide*, (London: HarperCollins, 1994).

Cecil C. Handisyde, *Everyday Details*, (London: Architectural Press, 1976).

David Harvey, *Consciousness and the Urban Experience*, (Oxford: Blackwell, 1985).

Rudolf Herz, editor *Ernst Neufert Architects' Data*, (UK: Granada Publishing, 1973).

Robert Hewison, *In Anger: British Culture in the Cold War 1945–60*, (New York: Oxford University Press, 1981).

M. Edgar Hoover and Raymond Vernon, *Anatomy of a Metropolis*, (USA: Harvard UP, 1959).

Penelope Houston, *The Contemporary Cinema*, (London: Penguin, 1963).

S. Humphries and J. Taylor, *The Making of Modern London 1945–1985*, (London: Sidgwick & Jackson, 1986).

Catherine Ingraham, 'Lines and Linearity Problems in Architectural Theory', in Andrea Kahn, editor, *Drawing Building Text*, (USA: Princeton Architectural Press, 1991).

Jane Jacobs, *The Death and Life of Great American Cities: The Failure of Town Planning*, (London, Penguin, 1965).

Henri Lefebvre, *The Explosion: Marxism and the French Revolution of May 1968*, (New York: Monthly Review, 1969).

Henri Lefebvre, *The Production of Space*, (Oxford: Blackwell, 1991).

Doris Lessing, *The Four Gated City*, (UK: Granada Publishing, 1972).

Ellen Lupton, *Mechanical Brides: Women and Machines from Home to Office*, (USA: Princeton University Press, 1993).

Sharon Marcus, 'Placing *Rosemary's Baby*', in *differences: A Journal of Feminist Cultural Studies*, (Providence, USA: Indiana University Press), Vol. 5, No. 3, pp. 121–53.

Arthur Marwick, *The Sixties*, (UK: Oxford University Press, 1998).

François Maspero, *Roissy Express*, (London: Verso, 1992).

Anne Massey, *The Independent Group – Modernism and Mass Culture in Britain 1945–1959*, (Manchester and New York: Manchester University Press, 1995).

Ministry of Housing and Local Government, *Homes for Today & Tomorrow*, (London: Her Majesty's Stationery Office, 1961).

C.C. Mead, *Charles Garnier's Paris Opera: Architectural Empathy and the Renaissance of French Classicism*, (Cambridge, Mass.: MIT Press, 1992).

Robert Murphy, *Sixties British Cinema*, (London: BFI Publishing, 1992).

Hermann Muthesius, *The English House*, edited by Dennis Sharp, (London: Crosby Lockwood Staples, 1979).

Joan Ockman, editor, *Architecture Culture 1943–1968*, (New York: Columbia Books on Architecture/Rizzoli, 1993).

Brendan O'Leary, 'British Farce, French Drama and Tales of Two Cities: Reorganisations of Paris and London Governments 1957–86', *London Public Administration*, v.65 (Winter 1987).

George Perry, *Forever Ealing: A Celebration of the Great British Film Studio*, (London: Pavilion Books, 1981).

Griselda Pollock, 'Modernity and the Spaces of Feminity', in *Vision and Difference: Feminity, Feminism and the Histories of Art*, (UK: Routledge, 1988).

Jonathan Raban, *Soft City*, (London: Hamish Hamilton, 1974).

S.E. Rasmussen, *London, The Unique City*, (USA/UK: MIT Press, 1982).

J.M. Richards, *The Castles on the Ground*, (London: The Architectural Press, 1946).

Richard Rogers and Mark Fisher, *A New London*, (London: Penguin, 1992).

Colin Rowe, 'Transparency: Literal and Phenomenal', *The Mathematics of the Ideal Villa and Other Essays*, (Cambridge, Mass.: MIT Press, 1982).

Jon Rowland, *Community Decay*, (London: Penguin, 1973).

George Rudé, *The Crowd in the French Revolution*, (UK: Oxford University Press, 1959).

Patrick Seale and Maureen McConville, *French Revolution 1968*, (London: Heinemann/ Penguin, 1968).

*The Shorter Oxford English Dictionary*, 3rd edition (USA: Guild Publishing, 1983).

William R. Taylor, *In Pursuit of Gotham City: Culture and Commerce in New York*, (New York: Oxford University Press, 1992).

Alain Touraine, *Le Mouvement de Mai ou le Communisme Utopique*, (Paris: Editions du Seuil, 1968).

P.L. Travers, *Mary Poppins in the Park*, (London: Peter Davies, 1962).

Vanity Fair, *Nice Girls Do: 'Vanity Fair's' Guide to the New Sexual Etiquette*, (USA: Hearst, 1971).

Mary and Neville Ward, *Home in the Twenties and Thirties*, (UK: Ian Allan Ltd, 1978).

F.R. Yerbury, editor, *Modern Homes Illustrated*, (London: Odhams Press, 1948).

Emile Zola, *Nana*, translation by George Holden, (London: Penguin, 1972).

# Acknowledgements

I thank: my partner Julian Williams for giving me the confidence to start writing in the first place, forcing the intellectual pace and ideas, originating the line of enquiry pursued in Chapter 4, and giving me time and space for this book; and my son Roman Akiba Williams, for his inspirational enthusiasm for the beauty of the everyday.

My mother, the late Zuzanna Shonfield, in particular for taking me round London's newest housing estates at the age of 13, and through her, the architects in my family: my great-grandfather, and architect of the main Warsaw synagogue, my cousin Boleslaw Eber, my great-uncle Juniek Sydenbeutel, and for passing on their enthusiasm for architecture and cities; my brother David Shonfield for introducing me to the serious side of popular culture on the terraces of Stamford Bridge; my late father, Andrew Akiba Shonfield for making me interested in trying out ideas; and the best of adoptive uncles, the late Alfred Hecht, for opening up the whole of modern art and post-war culture, and giving me financial help and encouragement to be a late starter.

Minna Thornton, James Lingwood, Kevin Rhowbotham, and Judith Williamson, who combined criticism, knowledge and intellectual generosity, and positively countered the negative impact of my secondary education over a great many years.

The residents of Grimaldi House including Hilary French, Ray Oxley and Paul Dart, but most especially John Sherwood, first for showing me that being an architecture student was more fun than working for a local authority, and second for helping me do it.

Colleagues at South Bank University who have provided the wherewithal to develop most of the ideas in this book: Marina Adams, Paul Davies for conversation and collaboration on the relationships of architecture and film, and the genesis of Brutalism, and Rose Nag. Jeremy Melvin and Nic Pople for non-stop support, P.G. Wodehouse quotes and an atmosphere of delightful enquiry. Professors Laurence Wood and Kit Allsopp for generously encouraging this work with interest and research time. Sandra Cracknell, Stan Lody and John Challis for exceptional combinations of technical expertise and flair with patience.

Muf Architects, especially Liza Fior, for testing opportunities, forcing issues, (including the writing of this book), and the trying out of ideas.

Frank O'Sullivan for provoking the creative and architectural interpretation of pollution taboo in our joint installation *Dirt is Matter Out of Place*.

I thank the following teachers who have been very important to me: Beatrice Mackewicz (Mrs Mack), Mrs Pringle, and Miss Johnson of Bousefield Primary School. Miss Johnson opened up a never-to-be-forgotten world of current affairs, modern art and maths to a group of 45 six year olds.

The teachers I have had since the age of 17, who repaired the intellectual damage wreaked by St Paul's Girls' School: Ruth Cole at Kingsway College for Further Education and all at the Department of Sociology, Kingston Polytechnic, especially Barry Sandywell.

An exceptional group of teachers at the Polytechnic of Central London (now the University of Westminster): Ralph Lerner, for the force of absolute encouragement combined with critical challenge; Lazlo Kiss, for encouragement at the time of my father's death; Eric Parry, for the tools to create an architectural world which could draw, positively, on the whole of experience; Robert Tavernor for confidence in manipulating an architectural language; Demetri Porphyrios for demonstrating critical method independent of stylistic taste; and David Greene's intellectual originality and patience which gave me a unique overview of my own work.

I had the good fortune to be taught by the late Robin Evans who supervised my dissertation. He had the rare capacity to make everyone taught by him feel special. I remember him whenever I write.

I thank Dalibor Vesely and Peter Carl at Cambridge for their intellectual generosity and erudition; my tutors at the Bartlett School, University College London, David Dunster, Iain Borden, and Adrian Forty who all enormously stimulated, criticised and encouraged the early stages of this work; Jonathan Hill for the opportunity to try out many of the ideas in the book for the first time on the third year students at the Bartlett, and for encouragement and discussion over the years. Edward Robbins at Harvard University for his active encouragement and support. Independent of any academic institution, Brendan Woods for being an exemplary mentor to an architectural apprentice: more than anyone he revealed to me the intellectual fascinations of building construction. Professor Derek Sugden for demonstrating in his work and thought the interweavings of architecture, engineering, literature and music, and Cedric Price for being a hero and a mensch.

Fellow students, now distinguished architects and academics, have taught me and given me generous help and encouragement. I especially thank: Anne Boddington, David Clews, Shaun Russell, Helen Springthorpe, Jeremy Till, Livia Tirone, Sarah Wigglesworth, and everyone in the self-taught, independent group of students at PCL called the Belfast Group in 1984–85. Among the many students I have taught, many also now distinguished architects, commentators and teachers, I particularly thank the following: at South Bank University, design students, Andrew Brook, Susan Connor, Paul Donaghey, Ray Emery, Paul Grover, Sarah Morrison, Suzie Murphy, Claud St Arroman, and Simon Whatley, who pressed me to use film as a basis for design studio in the first place; for their work on public space, Isabel Allen, Fay Chan and Dermot Brennan; Philip Dring for his work on *Beat Girl*, drawn on for Chapter 1, Damien Busch for his work on *Nana*, ideas drawn on in Chapters 4 and 5, and especially Katrin Dzenus and Tracy Chapman for their essay tracking parallels between the technology of sanitary protection and building technology, the inspiration behind the *Purity and Tolerance* installation at the Architecture Foundation with Muf Architects; and at the Bartlett, Katharina von Ledersteger, Almut Seeger, Christian Drosch and Yorg Ebers.

The unique work of Mark Cousins, Head of General Studies at the Architectural Association, is the inspiration behind much of the exploration in this book. He and the AA gave me an important platform to develop the initial ideas. I thank: Lee Mallett at *Building Design*; Paul Finch and Isabel Allen at the *Architects' Journal* – enlightened editors who have given me immense scope to try out ideas.

I should like to acknowledge the generosity and time of all the owners of copyrights used in this book, and in particular, John Herron, and all at Canal+ Image UK Limited, in acknowledgement of their great work in keeping British popular cultural heritage alive; Kevin Brownlow of Photoplay Productions Limited, and joint director of the inspirational *It Happened Here*, for his time and interest in this project; John Henderson at Euro London Films Limited, the Disney Corporation and Marie-Christine Belmotte at the Société Argos Film.

Finally, I want to thank the judges of the Anthony Pott Memorial Award, whose great generosity has allowed the publication of this book.

Chapter 1 was originally published as *Glossing with Graininess: Cross Occupations in Post-War British Film and Architecture* in *The Journal of Architecture* (London: Routledge, Winter 1998); the first part of Chapter 2 as *Purity and Tolerance – how building construction enacts pollution taboos* in AA Files 28 (London: Architectural Association, 1994), and the Endpiece as *The use of fiction to interpret architectural and urban space* in Iain Borden and Jane Rendell (eds), *InterSections: Architectural Histories and Critical Theories* (London: Routledge, 2000).

# Illustrations

**Chapter 3**

## Chapter 4

**Endpiece**

Every attempt has been made by the author to trace owners of the copyrights; however, in some cases it has not proved possible to either trace the owners or establish who owns copyright. In this case, all known information on ownership is provided above.

# Filmography

*Alfie* (U.K.: Paramount/Sheldrake, 1966) director: Lewis Gilbert.

*The Apartment* (U.S.A.: United Artists/Mirisch, 1960) director: Billy Wilder

*Beat Girl* (U.K.: Renown, 1960) director: Edmond T. Greville.

*The Chain* (Great Britain: 1984), director: Jack Gold

*Darling* (U.K.: Anglo-Amalgamated/Vic/Appia, 1965) director: John Schlesinger.

*La Dolce Vita* (Italy/France:1959) director: Federico Fellini.

*Four in the Morning* (Great Britain: West One, 1965), director: Anthony Simmons.

*Frenzy* (U.K.: Universal/Alfred Hitchcock,1972), director: Alfred Hitchcock.

*A Guide for the Married Man* (U.S.A.: TCF, 1967) director: Frank McCarthy.

*It Happened Here* (U.K.: United Artists/Kevin Brownlow, Andrew Mollo, 1963) directors: Kevin Brownlow and Andrew Mollo.

*Kind Hearts and Coronets* (U.K.: Ealing, 1949) director: Robert Hamer.

*L.A.Story* (U.S.A.: Guild/Rastar,1991), director: Mick Jackson.

*The Lavender Hill Mob* (Great Britain: Ealing, 1951), director: Charles Crichton.

*Mary Poppins* (U.S.A.:Walt Disney, 1964), director: Robert Stevenson.

*Passport to Pimlico* (U.K.:Ealing, 1949) director: Henry Cornelius.

*Repulsion* (U.K.: Compton/Tekli, 1965) director: Roman Polanski.

*Rosemary's Baby* (U.S.A.: Paramount/William Castle, 1968) director: Roman Polanski.

*Sabrina Fair* (U.S. title *Sabrina*) (U.S.A.: Paramount, 1954) director: Billy Wilder.

*Saturday Night and Sunday Morning* (U.K.: Bryanston/Woodfall, 1960) director: Karel Reisz.

*The Seven Year Itch* (U.S.A.: TCF, 1955), directors, Charles K. Feldman, Billy Wilder.

*This Sporting Life* (U.K.: Rank/Independent Artists, 1963) director: Lindsay Anderson.

*Two or Three Things I Know About Her* (France: Contemporary/Anouchka/ Argos/Les Films de Carosse/Parc Film, 1967) director: Jean-Luc Godard.

*A Taste of Honey* (U.K.: British Lion, 1961) director: Tony Richardson.

# Index